Overthinking

How to Rewire Your Brain, Control Your Thoughts, Emotions, Anxiety, Procrastination and Sleep. How to Gain Positive Habits, Mental Strength, Self-Confidence, Calmness and Serenity.

Matthew Wollkan

Table of Contents

Introduction **5**
Chapter 1: The Causes Of Overthinking **9**

   Low Self-Esteem 10
   Anxiety Disorder 15
   Depression Disorder 21

Chapter 2: How Overthinking Negatively Affects Your Life **26**

   How Do Negative Thoughts Affect A Person's Life Satisfaction? 26
   Increased Stress 27
   Symptom Checklist 28
   How Does Overthinking Affect A Person's Professional Development? 37
   How Does Overthinking Affect A Person's Relationships? 41

Chapter 3: The Benefits Of Overcoming Your Destructive Thoughts With Positivity **44**

Chapter 4: How To Control Your Anxiety **48**

   Understanding The Science Behind Anxiety And Overthinking 48
   Symptoms Of Anxiety And Overthinking 55
   Anxiety Management Techniques That Reduces Overthinking 65

Chapter 5: How To Manage Your Unhelpful Thoughts **75**

Unhelpful Thought Patterns 76
Challenging Your Unhealthy Thinking Patterns ... 79
Using Mindfulness Meditation To Control Your
Thoughts 83
Incorporating Mindfulness Into Your Life 85
Mindfulness Meditation Example Script 87
Incorporating Healthier Lifestyle Changes 93

Chapter 6: How Emotional Intelligence Will Help You 96

What Is Emotional Intelligence? 96
Self-Awareness 97
Self-Regulation 99
Motivation 100
Empathy 101
Social Skills 103
How Emotional Intelligence Benefits You 105
How To Increase Your Emotional Intelligence ... 108

Chapter 7: How Self-Discipline Will Help You 118

Improving Self-Discipline Is A Necessity 118
What Is The Driving Factor Behind Self-Discipline?
.... 119
How To Improve Your Self-Discipline (10-Step
Guide) 123
Changing Your Mindset Regarding Motivation ... 132
How To Stop Overthinking To Overcome
Procrastination 133

Chapter 8: The Role Your Subconscious Mind Plays 141

The Conscious Mind 141
The Subconscious Mind.. 141
The Inner Critic... 141

Chapter 9: Practical Methods To Stop Overthinking 146

Gratitude Practice 146
Talk To Yourself...147
Make an effort to find things to like, appreciate and love 148
Ask yourself the hard questions. 148
Practice affirmations 148

Conclusion 150

Introduction

Are you someone that overthinks the smallest decisions? Do you ever find yourself suddenly thinking that other people are perceiving you negatively due to small comments? Are you constantly afraid that your boss is going to fire you at any moment? Overthinking is a common problem that many people experience. The common misconception is that people think they may just be a chronic "overthinker" or that they just have a "bad habit." Neither of these justifications is true at all. In almost all cases, overthinking happens because of some form of anxiety disorder, depression disorder, or lack of self-esteem, which leads someone to overthink every little thing that happens to them. Some conditions that can cause chronic overthinking include; generalized anxiety disorder, social anxiety disorder, and depression. You have to understand that overthinking is likely a symptom of a mental health disorder like anxiety or depression. However, in certain cases, it can also be true that a person who naturally overthinks frequently can become diagnosed with a mental disorder like anxiety or depression. Just like the chicken and the egg, there's no way in telling which came first. Research points to the fact that overthinking is a symptom of mental disorders, but there still isn't enough evidence to eliminate the fact that it could be the other way around.

Overthinking is a major problem in our modern society. It is a big problem because mental health problems like anxiety are becoming an epidemic in North America. Did you know that anxiety disorders are the most common mental illnesses in the United States presently? It currently affects 40 million adults, which is 18% of the entire population. Anxiety disorders only began to be recognized in the 1980s. Before this, most professionals in the field would give a general diagnosis of 'stress' or 'nerves.' Since there were very little understanding and recognition of anxiety disorders, people who suffered from it received very little and effective treatment. Since then, we have come a long way in our research related to anxiety disorders. In the present day, we have solutions that range from behavioral therapy, talking therapies, meditation, and medication to help those who suffer from anxiety disorders to mitigate their overthinking.

Historically, humans have experienced anxiety since the barbaric days. Back in those days, anxiety was extremely helpful to protect us from dangerous situations. It is what triggers the fight or flight response. Anxiety is a basic emotion and is an experience that all species of animals experience. However, in the modern-day, anxiety has been hindering many people's lives.

In this book, we will be learning about all topics that are related to overthinking. We will first learn about the causes of overthinking to help you better identify the root of your own overthinking. You will then learn about what the effects of overthinking are, including its symptoms, overthinking as a symptom of anxiety/depression disorders, mental disorders that can cause overthinking and depression disorders that can cause overthinking. Once you've learned that, we will be exploring how you can relieve your anxiety to minimize your overthinking. In the later chapters, we will be studying ways of controlling your mind to manage better and minimize negative and overthinking thoughts. I will teach you how you can use scientific-based therapies such as Cognitive Behavioral Therapy and many others to identify unhealthy thinking patterns and help you challenge and change any negative thoughts or emotions.

Later on in this book, I will teach you about how meditation will help reduce overthinking. I will also teach you how making improvements to your physical health can lower a person's negativity, and how bettering your emotional intelligence can help you understand your thoughts and emotions. Those who overthink frequently tend to lack motivation, which prevents them from achieving their goals. I will teach you how you can improve your self-discipline and self-confidence to overcome negativity and achieve the goals you have always wanted to achieve. Learning about these things will include learning about how to overcome procrastination. I will wrap up this book by teaching you the different strategies that help with controlling overthinking. Throughout this book, you will be provided with many real-world examples to illustrate how you can combat overthinking.

Battling with overthinking is a battle that never ends. You need to constantly be vigilant with analyzing your thoughts and identifying when bouts of anxiety begin to occur. When it does, you need to redirect your thoughts to prevent overthinking. This book will teach you how to identify the unhealthy thinking patterns you have and how to change your thought process, so it doesn't lead to the emotion of anxiety. By being able to manage and monitor your thoughts, you will, in turn, be able to control your emotions, which then affects your behavior.

Typically, overthinking is not a disorder or problem on its own and is more of a symptom of another larger issue. As mentioned, overthinking is a common symptom of low self-esteem, anxiety, and depression. This book will focus on the different areas of your life that can cause you to overthink. Understanding these areas will help you better understand where your overthinking is coming from. Understanding the actual cause of your specific overthinking will help you narrow down the strategies you can use to start mitigating this problem. When a person gets caught in a cycle of overthinking, it begins to affect all areas of their life, which usually prevents them from achieving the goals they want to achieve. Those who overthink have more trouble making decisions and thus cause a lot of procrastination in their lives. When procrastination is a dominant part of someone's life, it is difficult for them to accomplish goals and, therefore, causes them to have lower life satisfaction. Without further ado, let's get started.

Chapter 1: The Causes Of Overthinking

Understanding how overthinking works and what is causing that to happen to you is the first step for you to control your thoughts and stop your own overthinking. In its simplest form, overthinking is the process of constantly analyzing and anguishing over your thoughts. It can sometimes include rumination. Rumination is when a person gets stuck in the cycle of reliving their past or present experiences and actions. Although many people think that overthinking is a separate disorder, it often happens because of a mental disorder like anxiety or depression. A common symptom of anxiety that patients report is the tendency to overthink every little action they want to perform. However, overthinking can also be the byproduct of low self-esteem. You need to recognize where your overthinking problems stem from.

This chapter will teach you about the three main causes of overthinking; self-esteem, anxiety, and depression. If you are feeling alone in this, don't. Overthinking is a common problem that people face, and it comes about by one of the three reasons mentioned above, which plagues our society today. Overthinking makes it difficult to live life to the fullest and often impacts your emotional and physical health. Understanding where your overthinking is coming from is the first step in the right direction.

Low Self-Esteem

A person's self-esteem fluctuates throughout their life, depending on their circumstances or stage of life. It is not ordinary to have moments where a person feels down about themselves and not strange to have moments where they feel good about themselves. However, if a person is suffering from low self-esteem, it often causes them to doubt themselves and their ability. When this happens, it causes the person to have a vicious cycle where they overthink every little decision or thought they have as they always want to make the 'right' choice or the 'correct' decision.

Generally, a person's self-esteem stays within a range that relates directly to their opinion of themselves and increases as a person gets older. The range here is low self-esteem to high self-esteem. Healthy self-esteem is located right in between the two extremes.

The ideal level here is to have self-esteem somewhere in the middle and not aim to have 'high' self-esteem. Extreme high self-esteem is called boasting and often is just a cover-up for having low self-esteem. However, for our purposes, let's consider high self-esteem as it's own extreme and not just another type of low self-esteem. In this chapter, you will be determining whether or not you think self-esteem is the cause of your overthinking.

The people who don't value their thoughts and opinions tend to have low self-esteem. They often don't focus on their skills and credit that they deserve but instead focuses on their past mistakes and perceived weaknesses. They tend to have the mindset that other people are better or more capable than them. They also struggle with accepting positive feedback. They find themselves afraid of failure, which prevents them from trying to do things and, ultimately, holds them back from success. The fear of failure is what typically causes a person with low self-esteem to overthink every little decision and interaction in their life.

Below is a checklist of symptoms showcased in a person who has low self-esteem. Please check off the ones you think you exhibit. If you check off four or more boxes, you are likely to have low self-esteem.

❏
You experience regular anxiety.

❏
You often feel depressed.

❏
You always put the needs of other people before your own.

❏
You often feel ashamed.

❏
You are doubtful in your ability to reach success.

❏
You choose the wrong partners for you.

❏
You criticize other people often.

- [ ] You are afraid of being alone.
- [ ] You become rigid.

Arguably, people with high self-esteem are trying to cover up for the fact that they have low self-esteem. High self-esteem is very different from healthy self-esteem because healthy self-esteem does not exhibit conceitedness or cockiness. People with healthy self-esteem exhibit traits opposite to that like humility and modesties. Rather than earning respect from others, those with high self-esteem don't respect themselves enough, so they need to make up for it by over-communicating their strengths and skills to get others to show them the respect they want. In other words, this is overcompensation.

Even though high self-esteem people have low self-esteem, they tend to have behaviors that differ from those with low self-esteem. To put things simply, individuals with low self-esteem do not believe in their capabilities when it comes to accomplishing tasks and therefore shies away from most things or relies on others to do it for them. Individuals with high self-esteem similarly also don't believe in their capabilities of accomplishing tasks and also shies away from it. Still, they don't hide their inabilities by avoiding the task. Instead, they hide it by the usage of words to brag about their skills and abilities. There is a clear difference here.

Individuals that have healthy self-esteem do not usually exhibit the behaviors of bragging or boasting. Instead, these people have confidence when they are speaking about a topic that they have accomplishments. Those with high self-esteem often bring up parts of their life intending to brag about them. They do this to mask their low self-esteem in other parts of their life. For instance, person A with healthy self-esteem may say, "After two years of training for the triathlon and failing the past couple times, I finally was able to finish it! I am now training for the next 20 weeks for the Iron Man competition." Person A is expressing how proud they feel regarding the work that they have put into their success without leaving out the obstacles they faced during their journey.

On the contrary, person B with low self-esteem may sound like this "I only trained for six months and finished the triathlon while other people take years to train for it! I bet I could've done it without any training at all." The difference in the statement that person B made is that they are not talking about the obstacles and failures that they have faced along the way. We know that avoiding failure is impossible, so their statement is likely not truthful. They also focused on comparing themselves with other people, where a person with a healthy self-esteem doesn't compare their achievements with others.

Below is another checklist of behaviors. This time it is showcasing the behaviors of a person with high self-esteem. Check off the ones that apply to you.

❏
You notice some people seem put off at work, and you suspect it may be due to you acting overly conceited.

❏
You find that you are more concerned with your skills and performance and are not involved with your partner's at all.

❏
You often don't take on projects or opportunities because you think they are too "easy," or you deem them as beneath your abilities.

❏
You take on too many projects when you fully know that you don't have the skills to finish all of them.

❏
You often notice some distance between you and some of your friends and suspect that it may come from your possible arrogance.

Where did you score on the self-esteem scale? If you either scored low or high in self-esteem, then your overthinking is likely caused by this. Later on in this book, you will be taught numerous strategies that can help you boost your self-confidence and foster a more positive mindset to stop overthinking so frequently.

Keep in mind that your overthinking can have multiple causes. Your overthinking symptoms can be a combination of low self-esteem and other types of mental disorders. Continue reading the following chapters to identify if your overthinking has more than one cause.

Anxiety Disorder

Overthinking is one of the most common symptoms of anxiety. The more anxious a person is, the more likely they are to over-analyze every little piece of information before taking action. When a person is anxious, they normally have developed unhealthy thinking patterns, which causes them to have negative thoughts come up in their mind at inopportune moments.

If this happens to you, it is a form of self-defense that your brain employs to help you prepare for a potential disaster. Unfortunately, these negative thinking patterns are learned and can go haywire, meaning that it causes negative thoughts even though there is no imminent threat.

As we learned in this chapter, it is hard to tell whether overthinking causes mental disorders like anxiety and depression or if it's anxiety and depression that causes overthinking. Regardless of the answer, it is important to understand both causes to understand your overthinking source better. In this subchapter, we will be learning about two anxiety disorders that are a common culprit of causing overthinking. Generalized Anxiety Disorder and social anxiety disorder are two disorders that frequently cause a person to overthink every little action they perform. Let's take a look at what each of them is.

Generalized Anxiety Disorder (GAD)

Generalized anxiety is the susceptibility to excessive panic, worry, overthinking, or anxiety regarding numerous events or situations. Usually, the person has major difficulty controlling their feelings of worry and is associated with other symptoms such as fatigue, restlessness, concentration difficulties, sleep disturbance, irritability, and muscle tension. We define the feeling of worry as; a process focused on the uncertainty of future events' outcomes. It is not an emotion itself, but it leads to feeling the emotion of anxiety. The main and most obvious symptom of generalized anxiety disorder is the "what if" thoughts that begin to occur. These "what if" thoughts work hand in hand with worrying, and it often feels like it is uncontrollable. Also, the process of worry is often associated with physical symptoms that are related to the flight or fight response. It often happens that the individual will think of the future negatively and have thoughts that are followed by feelings of anxiety.

People with GAD often feel worried and anxious most of the time and not just in specific stressful situations. The worries that they have been constant, intense, and interferes with their daily routine. Their worries are typically multiple aspects and not only one. It may include work, health, finance, family, or just everyday life things. Trivial tasks such as household chores or being late for a meeting can lead to extreme anxiety, leading to doom.

Most people are diagnosed with GAD if they showcase some of the symptoms for six months or more:

- You feel extremely worried about numerous activities or events.
- You struggle to stop worrying.
- You are finding that your anxiety has made it very hard for you to do your daily routine (e.g., studying, working, hanging out with friends)
- You constantly feel restless or on edge.
- You are always/easily tired.
- You struggle with concentration.
- You are easily irritable.
- You have tension in your muscles (e.g., neck or sore jaw)
- You struggle with sleeping (e.g., difficulty staying asleep or falling asleep)

So what exactly causes GAD? This one is tricky; there is a combination of different factors that take place. First, we must consider biological factors. Certain changes in brain functions come along with GAD. Next, we also take family history into account. Often, people who have GAD have a history of mental health issues in their family. Stressful life events also increase the risk of someone developing GAD. For example, loss of a relationship, moving, or physical or emotional abuse are all examples of events that can play a role in causing GAD. Lastly, psychological factors may also put a person at higher risk. Those who have personality traits of being sensitive, nervous, or inability to tolerate frustration are at higher risk of GAD.

Social Anxiety

Although it is very normal to feel a certain level of nervousness in social situations, it is not normal to feel overwhelming anxiety. Situations such as attending formal events, public speaking, and doing presentations are likely events in which you feel nervous and anxious. However, for those who suffer from social anxiety (or otherwise known as social phobia), speaking or performing in front of other people and general social situations can lead to extreme anxiety. This extreme anxiety usually stems from the fear of being criticized, judged, humiliated, or laughed at in front of other people. A lot of the time, they are afraid of trivial and ordinary matters. For example, those who suffer from social anxiety may feel that eating at a restaurant around other people can be extremely daunting.

Social anxiety usually occurs during the lead up to performance events (e.g., having to give a speech or working while people are watching them) and situations where social interaction is involved (e.g., having lunch with coworkers or normal small talk). Social anxiety also occurs during the actual event, as well as the lead-up. Moreover, this type of phobia can also be very specific where the individual fears a specific situation. For example, they can be fearful of having to be assertive during work meetings.

The symptoms of social anxiety include psychological and physical symptoms. People with social phobia find it very distressing when they experience physical symptoms. These physical symptoms include:

- Excessive perspiration
- Nausea/Diarrhea
- Trembling
- Stammering, stuttering, or blushing when speaking

When these physical symptoms occur, it normally causes the anxiety to increase as the person begins to fear that other people will notice these signs. However, these signs are usually not noticeable to other people. Those who suffer from this condition say that they also excessively worry that they will say or do something wrong, which will lead to a terrible result.

Often, people with social anxiety will attempt to avoid situations where they feel like they may act in an embarrassing or humiliating way. If they can't avoid certain situations, they will choose to endure it but will become very distressed and anxious and try to exit that situation as fast as possible. Leaving situations abruptly in this way can begin to affect their relationships negatively. Moreover, it may begin to affect their professional lives and their ability to maintain their daily routine.

Doctors will typically base a social anxiety diagnosis on having the symptoms mentioned above and how much distress and impairment causes the individual's day-to-day routine. Usually, if symptoms continue for six months, a doctor will likely diagnose them with social anxiety.

Some social phobia symptoms that are psychological include:

- You feel extreme nervousness before performing in front of other people.
- You feel extreme nervousness before meeting unfamiliar people.
- You feel extreme nervousness or embarrassment when being observed (e.g., eating or drinking in front of others, talking on the phone in front of others)
- You avoid going to certain events or interactions due to the fear of social nervousness.
- You have difficulty going about daily life (e.g., studying, seeing friends, and working)

Research suggests that 11% of the population has experienced social anxiety in their lifetime. It showed that women experience this disorder more than men. A lot of the time, this phobia starts during childhood or adolescence.

So, what exactly causes social anxiety? There are numerous causes, but the most common ones are temperament, family history, and learned behavior.

When it comes to temperament, children or adolescents who are shy are at more risk than others. Specifically, for children, those who exhibit shyness and timidity puts them at risk of developing social anxiety in their adulthood. Family history is also a possibility when it comes to cause due to genetic predisposition. The main cause, however, is usually learned behavior. Often, those who suffer from social anxiety develop this condition due to being treated poorly, embarrassed in public, or humiliated. Socially anxious people also tend to overthink every little interaction they have with others, both before, during, and after the interaction.

Depression Disorder

Overthinking is also a symptom of depression. Those who are depressed likely suffer from having low self-esteem and therefore are more prone to questioning every little action they make before actually making it. Depression is a tricky mental disorder as it manifests differently, depending on the individual. If you suspect that your overthinking is a symptom of a depression disorder, please make sure to see a licensed health professional get a diagnosis properly. This visit will help you find the best solutions to treat your disorder, ranging from therapy, medication, and meditation.

Depression has a sneaky way of causing its victims to begin overthinking. Many people with depression report that they constantly doubt their own ability to achieve tasks. They report that they find themselves overthinking every little action before gathering the courage to perform that task. Just like anxiety, there is no way of finding out whether it's the overthinking that came first or the depression disorder that causes it. All we can do is learn about what these are so you can identify what the source of your overthinking is. Let's take a look at different types of depression disorders that can cause overthinking.

Mild/Moderate Depression

The most common types of depression are mild and moderate depression. This type of depression is more than just feeling 'sad' or 'blue.' The symptoms of this type of depression often interfere with people's lives by robbing them of motivation and joy, causing them to overthink. These symptoms can feel amplified in moderate depression and often lower a person's self-esteem and self-confidence.

A type of 'low-grade' depression is called dysthymia. When a person has dysthymia, they feel mild to moderately depressed more often than not, but they do have brief periods of feeling a normal mood. Here are some defining traits of dysthymia:

- Symptoms of dysthymia are not as severe or strong as the symptoms of major depression, but they do tend to last for a long time (minimum of 2 years)
- Some people report that they experience intense depressive episodes on top of having

dysthymia; this is a condition called 'double depression.'
- When a person is suffering from dysthymia, they may feel like they have always been depressed for their whole lives. They may think that their consistent low mood is 'just the way they are.'

Chronic/Major Depression

Major depression is a less common form of mild or moderate depression; severe and relentless symptoms characterize it. Here are two characteristics of major depression:

- If major depression is left untreated, it usually lasts for about six months
- Although some people only experience one depressive episode in their life, major depression can be a disorder that is recurring throughout their life

Atypical Depression

Atypical depression is a subtype of major depression that is very common that has specific symptom patterns. It has a better response with some medications and therapies than others, identifying this type of depression is very helpful when it comes to prescribing treatment. Here are a few traits to describe it further:

- Generally, people who ave atypical depression experience a temporary increase in their mood when they experience positive events. These events could include hanging out with friends or receiving some sort of good news.
- Atypical depression includes increased appetite, weight gain, sleeping excessively, sensitivity to rejection, and a 'heavy feeling' in their arms and legs.

Seasonal Affective Disorder (SAD)

Although many people think this type of depression is just a myth, it is a real condition. When they experience reduced daylight hours during winter, some people can cause them to form a type of depression called seasonal affective disorder (SAD). Although this is not a popular type of depression, SAD affects 1% - 2% of the general population, predominantly young people and women. SAD can make a person feel completely different from the person they are in the summer. People tend to feel stressed, sad, hopeless, tense and have little interest in friends or activities they normally enjoy. SAD usually begins during Autumn or Winter, where the days are short and remains until Spring's brighter days come along.

In conclusion, the disorders that I've highlighted above are the main culprits of a person's overthinking. Is there a disorder that you just read about that you feel like you relate to? If you feel like this is the case, it will be beneficial for you to seek a health professional to get properly diagnosed.

Chapter 2: How Overthinking Negatively Affects Your Life

We know that overthinking harms all areas of your life. However, to make matters worse, if your overthinking leads to negative thoughts, it can cause many undesirable effects on your body and with your relationships. In this chapter, I will teach you some of the effects that negative overthinking has on your overall life satisfaction, relationships, and professional life. You will learn that one of the main effects of overthinking is stress. If stress is left untreated, it can cause many other issues for you that maybe even more difficult to resolve. Moreover, overthinking is also a major cause of procrastination, which will also play a role in your ability to achieve goals and get important tasks done, thus causing more stress.

How Do Negative Thoughts Affect A Person's Life Satisfaction?

Negative thinking highly affects a person's life satisfaction. This lowered life satisfaction is generally due to the stress that is caused by constant negative and repeating thoughts. To better understand how this affects a person, let's dive a little bit deeper into the effects of stress and its symptoms.

Increased Stress

Numerous experts worldwide agree that the misconception of stress only being a psychological feeling is very dangerous. They used an analogy to explain this further. Since the human stress response has evolved over the millions of years, it originally helped our ancestors identify danger and food. This feeling is very natural; without it, humans would befriend bears rather than gathering berries from forests. There are a lot of threats back in those days that range from avoiding predators to finding food. This reaction is completely natural, and without our stress response, we would've never made it this far. However, what isn't natural is how modern life exposes us to milder threats, but our stress is constant. This stress happens from being overwhelmed with stimulation, juggling too many things, multitasking, and being always on the go. Humans are not meant to run away from predators for 10+ hours per day without any breaks in simpler terms. Essentially, this is what humans are doing in modern-day society.

Many experts have named the common condition of chronic stress in our society as the "super stress." Humans are now being overwhelmed with numerous stressors that we almost take for granted. These stressors include; inadequate salaries, job dissatisfaction, being overworked, not having enough time for family and friends, lack of time outside, noise pollution, and feeling like their life has no purpose or meaning. The crazy part about all of this is that our body cannot physically differentiate between being attacked by a bear and getting a bad job review. The chemical and biological response in our body is the same. Due to this, the body begins to get worn down due to the intensity of the stress.

When people are constantly in a state of stress all day, they overuse every element of their bodies. The result is a series of stress symptoms. Some people's stress can get so bad that it evolves from simply being 'annoying' into debilitating. Many people can develop other mental disorders when under too much stress, such as; anxiety and depression. Let's take a look into what is happening with our biochemistry when we are stressed out.

Symptom Checklist

Although stress shows itself in different ways, depending on the individual, there are a few common symptoms that most people experience. By understanding the symptoms related to stress, you will become an expert at identifying when experiencing it. When you find yourself experiencing stress, it is probably an effect of your overthinking. When you feel stressed, try to think back and see if you were overthinking before the feelings of stress arose. An important part of stress management is identifying triggers and stressors. To do this, you need to know what symptoms you show when you're stressed and figure out when they occur. Please take a look at this detailed checklist below:

❏ Acne

One of the most visible ways that stress shows itself in a person is through acne. When people are under a lot of stress, they have the tendency to touch their faces with their hands frequently, which causes bacteria to spread into their pores, which develops cane. Scientific studies have also confirmed that high levels of stress cause a higher risk of acne. To be specific, one of these studies measured a group of people's level of acne before and during a school exam. At the end of the study, they found that they developed more severe acne when people had increased levels of stress. A similar study focused on teenagers found that worse acne was also associated with stress levels, particularly in boys. Although these studies show a strong association between stress levels and acne, it doesn't consider other factors that may be playing a role. More research in this area is needed to prove the connection further. Besides stress, acne can be caused by; blocked pores, excess oil production, bacteria, and hormonal shifts.

❏ Headaches

Just like acne, many scientific studies have found a relationship between high levels of stress and headaches. The definition of headaches includes pain that is in the head or neck region. One scientific study that tested this relationship consisted of around 250 people that were suffering from chronic headaches. The scientists found that within those people, 45% of them had recently endured a stressful event. A similar but larger study found an increase in stress intensity led to increased headaches over one month. If that's not enough evidence, another similar study focused on 150 military professionals at a clinic specialized for headaches. They found that nearly 70% of those who had headaches said that they are stress-induced. This result makes stress the second most common trigger for headaches. Lastly, other common triggers of headaches can include dehydration, alcohol consumption, and lack of sleep.

❏ Chronic Pain

People commonly report that they have an increased amount of pains and aches in their bodies when they are under a lot of stress. One study that focused on this relationship consisted of about 40 people that had sickle cell disease. They found that when they had increased levels of stress daily, they felt an increase in pain as well. Another study focused on studying cortisol, the stress hormone, and how it is also associated with chronic pain levels. For instance, a study consisted of 16 people who reported having chronic back pain. When they studied them further, they found that these people had high levels of cortisol. Another similar study found that people who reported having chronic pain had higher cortisol levels within their hair. High cortisol levels are an indicator of someone who has been under prolonged stress. Again, bear in mind that these studies have shown relationships between stress and chronic pain, but we still have to consider other factors that could play a role.

Moreover, it is still unsure whether chronic pain causes stress or if stress causes chronic pain. This chronic pain symptom is something that still needs to be further studied. Several other factors could be playing a role in increasing chronic pain, such as; nerve damage, poor posture, injuries, and age.

❑ Frequent Sickness

If you feel like you are always sick, or always battling allergies or a case of sniffles, stress can be the culprit. Stress takes a huge toll on people's immune systems, which will put you at a higher risk of infections. In a recent study, scientists gave a group of 60 adults in the flu vaccine. They found that the people who had a weakened response to that vaccine indicated that stress is related to decreased immunity. In a similar study, over 200 adults were selected and split into two groups; low stress and high stress. Throughout six months, 70% of the people that were in the high-stress group experienced respiratory infections. They also had 60% more symptoms of the illness compared to the low-stress group. In addition to this study, another similar study showed that a person's increased susceptibility to developing a respiratory illness was linked to increased stress levels. Again, more of these relationships still require further research as the connection between stress and immunity is complex. Although stress is related to a person's immune health, it can also happen along with other factors such as multiple myeloma, leukemia, physical inactivity, and a poor diet.

❏ Insomnia And Decreased Energy

When a person is under high levels of prolonged stress, they can begin to feel that they have decreased energy levels and chronic fatigue. For instance, a study of over 2000 participants reported that tiredness and constant fatigue was in fact, associated with high-stress levels. Stress also affects a person's sleep cycle and could cause insomnia, which could be the cause of fatigue. A small study found that people who had high levels of stress-related to work were associated with restlessness before bed and increased sleepiness throughout the day. Another study that also consisted of over 2000 2000 participants found that people who experienced higher numbers of stressful events were associated with an increased risk of insomnia. Like other symptoms, these studies show a relationship, but they may not be accounting for other factors that may cause the symptom. More research in this area is required to define the relationship between stress and fatigue directly. Other factors that can cause fatigue include; underactive thyroid, a poor diet, low blood sugar, and dehydration.

❏ Decreased Libido

Numerous people experience a change in their sex drive when they are going through a stressful time. A small study that focused on 30 women evaluated their stress levels and then had them watch an erotic film to measure their arousal. The women that had higher levels of stress reported less arousal compared to those that were less stressed. A similar study that was larger consisted of about 100 women that found that high levels of stress directly contributed to their lower levels of sexual satisfaction and activity. A similar study focused on over 300 participants and found that the people who reported high-stress levels found that their sexual satisfaction, arousal, and desire got negatively impacted. Again, you must also consider other factors that may be contributing to a person's changing libido. These factors could include psychological causes, fatigue, and hormonal changes.

❏ Digestive Issues

When people experience higher levels of stress, they tend to have problems with their digestive system, such as constipation and diarrhea. In one study, they had nearly 3000 children that participated, and they found that when they experienced stressful events, they had an increased risk of constipation. Stress also affects people who already have digestive disorders such as inflammatory bowel disease (IBD) or irritable bowel syndrome (IBS). These two disorders share traits such as constipation, diarrhea, bloating, and stomach pain. In another study of almost 200 women, they found that having high daily stress levels lead to an increase in their digestive distress. An overall analysis that focused on 18 different studies that explored the relationship between stress and digestive diseases found that almost 75% of these studies have found a relationship between a person's digestive system and stress levels. We have to keep in mind that although these studies show a strong association, more studies are required to look at how stress impacts a person's digestive system. Other factors can also cause digestive issues such as; medications, infections, physical activity levels, dehydration, and diet.

❑ Appetite Changes

One of the most commonly reported symptoms of stress is a change in a person's appetite. When people are feeling stressed out, they often showcase one of two extremes:

- They raid their fridge in the middle of the night.
- They experience a complete loss of appetite and have no desire to eat.

A scientific study that focused on college students found that around 80% found that they had appetite changes when they were under high stress. Out of this population of students, nearly 40% experienced a decrease in appetite, while around 60% reported an increased appetite. In a similar study of around 100 people, they found that these people, when under stress, exhibited behaviors like eating even when they are not hungry. Weight fluctuations can also cause a person's change in appetite during high-stress times. For instance, a study of over 1000 people found that weight gain in overweight adults occurred along with stress. Although these studies show a strong association between the change in a person's appetite and stress levels and weight, more studies must further understand what other factors could be involved. Other factors include; psychological conditions, hormonal shifts, drugs, or certain medications.

❑ Depression

Certain studies suggest that the development of depression is related to chronic stress. One study that looked at around 800 women who had depression found that the beginning stages of their depression were heavily linked to chronic or acute stress. Another study discovered that higher levels of depressive symptoms were associated with increased levels of stress. This study consisted of around 200 adolescents. In another study, around 40 people who had major depression found that their depressive episodes were related to stressful life events. Keep in mind that these studies have shown associations between depression and stress, but it does not mean that every case of depression is caused by it. We must do a lot more research on this topic to 100% confirm the role that stress plays in depression. Other factors that aren't stress that contribute to depression include; certain medications, environmental factors, hormone levels, and family history.

❏ Rapid Heartbeat

Symptoms of high-stress levels often include an increased heart rate or a fast heartbeat. One study that found an association between stress and rapid heartbeats discovered that a person's heart rate is much higher when going through a stressful situation. Another similar study focused on about 100 teenagers, and they discovered that an increase in heart rate was caused by undergoing a stressful task. Another similar study exposed about 90 students to stressful tasks and found that they had increased blood pressure and heart rates. Interestingly, however, they found that playing relaxing and soothing music during that task prevented a rapid heartbeat. An increased heartbeat can also result from other factors such as drinking alcohol, caffeine, heart conditions, thyroid disease, and high blood pressure.

❏ Sweating

When a person is under a lot of stress, it can cause them to sweat excessively. A small study that consisted of 20 participants who had a condition caused them to have excessive sweating in their palms. This study monitored their sweating rate throughout the day using a scale of 0 – 10. They found that stress and exercise both increased the sweating rate significantly by 2 to 5 points. Another study discovered that it also resulted in more sweating and odor within 40 teenage participants when they experience stress. Other factors that can cause excessive sweating include; medications, thyroid conditions, heat exhaustion, and anxiety.

How Does Overthinking Affect A Person's Professional Development?

When a person has a negative mind that is constantly overthinking everything, it tends to cause a lot of stress and anxiety in their workplace. Deadlines feel a lot tighter, and your work feels less meaningful. When a person has a negative outlook on their work, anxieties rise, and work becomes more stressful, causing more anxiety. It's a vicious cycle. Let's take a look at the stressors that can arise from work due to negative overthinking and some causes of overthinking at work.

Overthinking has been found to cause financial problems. With the cost of living going up in many big cities, people are often finding that their salary simply doesn't cut it. Struggling financially and having to stress about which bill they prioritize to pay over another is a huge facet of worry in someone's life.

Moreover, the job market isn't exactly booming, so finding a new job that pays more isn't an option for most people. They may begin to have anxieties or worries regarding how they're going to make ends meet, which dominates their mind and festers into anxiety. This anxiety creates more negative thoughts regarding their work, likely due to feeling like their effort isn't fairly compensated.

Secondly, overthinking can lead to people having career crises. A career crisis could mean not getting the promotion you were looking for or feeling like your career does not align with your goals and aspirations. This feeling can cause a huge disruption in your happiness at work, which may lead to having anxiety about going to work as you may feel like you are spending your time but going nowhere with it. Since you are at work for most of your day, if not entirely, feeling unhappy at work takes a toll on people's wellbeing, which leads to having anxiety about going back somewhere that makes you unhappy.

Moreover, overthinking mixed with a workplace culture shift can cause many issues. Workplaces with bad culture can be extremely mentally exhausting for most people. Bad workplace culture often causes anxiety before going into work as you are dreading to have to tolerate your workplace culture. In this situation, many people often feel like they cannot leave or find a new job as their current workplace may make them feel undervalued and undesirable to any other company. People often prioritize working in a place with a good culture over money or career growth in their job hunts. Bad workplace culture fuels negative feelings towards it even more.

Also, long commutes constantly prove to cause overthinking and stress in many people. Having a long commute is frequently identified as one of the biggest stressors of work. Since most people work a standard 40-hour workweek (if not more), throwing in a 1 hour + commute each way and back begins to drain a person's liveliness. Being gone to work for at least a minimum of 10 hours a day does not leave a person much time or energy to practice things like self-care, exercise, or doing their hobbies. Their life begins to revolve around going to work, and work itself. Without a work-life balance, many people find that they begin to feel anxious regarding their happiness and well-being as they don't have the time to care for themselves properly.

The type of work that a person is doing can affect their levels of stress and overthink. Depending on what type of work you are doing, you may feel added stress or anxieties. For example, a nurse working in the emergency room may have to handle more stressful situations than someone working as a receptionist at a massage clinic. When people constantly experience stressful situations at work, it drains their energy mentally more than anything else. This experience can cause anxieties about going to work, performing well at work, and trying to find the energy to do other things in their life.

Similarly, unfulfilling work can cause the same negative impacts too. Unfulfilling work promotes negativity in many people. For example, although a doctor may have a more stressful and anxiety-inducing job, he/she may find pleasure or fulfillment in helping people and saving lives. This reward may be what keeps them going through stressful times. However, someone with a sales job may have high stress due to the targets implemented on them do not necessarily feel any fulfillment in their work. When someone is highly stressed and dissatisfied, they begin to worry about their happiness and ultimately manifest into anxiety about their life and work. This worry and anxiety are why people often take a pay cut and leave a stressful and unfulfilling job for something that may pay less but is either more fulfilling or less stressful.

Now that you have learned some effects that negative overthinking has on work, it is important to understand some of these symptoms. If you think you are suffering from workplace anxiety, take a look at yourself and assess if you are displaying any of the following symptoms:

- A desire to be perfect
- Feeling like you are going "crazy"
- Constant worrying
- Feeling irritable
- Trouble sleeping
- Avoiding family/friends
- Over/under eating
- Bad memory

- Muscle tension
- Loss of interest in your work
- Difficulties in Concentration
- Crying
- Feeling down
- Tiredness
- Irrational fear of making mistakes

How Does Overthinking Affect A Person's Relationships?

Negativity and overthinking during relationships cause a variety of problems. Not only is the relationship less likely to be successful, but important factors like sex are also affected. Negativity and overthinking tend to cause a lot of anxiety within both partners, and anxiety has negatively affected a person's sex life. Let's look at the negative effects of negativity and anxiety on a person's sex life.

Not only can negativity hold you back in the workplace and create more stress levels for you in general, the worry, fear, and apprehension that comes with it may cause some stress in your sex life as well. According to researchers in the sex and relationship field, all anxiety and negativity is a distraction when it comes to sexual success. Let's learn about how anxiety can affect different aspects of your sex life.

Overthinking has been found to lower a person's libido. Feelings of negativity and anxiety can lower your sex drive in multiple ways. The feeling of being overwhelmed during bouts of anxiety could dominate your mind and push thoughts about sex out of your brain, which prevents you from getting in the mood even if you were feeling it earlier in your day. The actions of panic and worry also play a big physical effect on your body as it ramps up the production of stress hormones (e.g., adrenaline) that causes you to feel uneasy or on edge. When you have trouble relaxing your physical body, experience sexual sensations, and reach orgasm can be very difficult.

Also, overthinking lowers a person's level of body confidence. Getting naked in front of another person is often nerve-wracking for most people, even if you have gotten naked in front of this person numerous times before! However, when you are struggling with anxiety, you are more likely to feel self-conscious and obsess over your "body flaws". Same with men and women, both genders can be very self-conscious regarding their body shape, type, or a particular body part. When you are feeling anxious or negative, that feeling of self-consciousness becomes heightened. When people are continually critical of themselves due to shaming their own body, they turn off their ability to receive sexual pleasure and struggle with being fully emotionally present and physically present during sex.

Overthinking can also cause intimacy difficulties. When someone constantly feels panic and fear, they may not want to be emotionally or physically close to anyone, even their partner. For those who may have suffered from past trauma, sexual touch, or sex itself can be anxiety-inducing and scary. When a person feels triggered by the reminder of past trauma or negative events, it can cause their body to shut down fully and prevent any arousal experience from being pleasurable enough for the climax. If a person does not realize this, the individual may begin to avoid sex or any type of foreplay, causing a strain on the relationship.

Furthermore, overthinking has been found to lead to orgasm struggles. Anxiety often has symptoms that include shallow breathing and clenched muscles, which also play a huge role in preventing a person from letting go and achieving orgasm. The condition of anxiety can raise an individual's 'orgasmic threshold'. This term means how long and how much stimulation a person requires to reach an orgasm. If the person is a woman, anxiety can also prevent the body from making lubrication, making their body uncomfortable and can trigger vaginismus, which is a disorder that makes your vaginal muscles very tense to a point where penetration is not possible. These physical changes, combined with anxiety and a negative mind, can mess up a person's awareness of sexual stimulation.

Chapter 3: The Benefits Of Overcoming Your Destructive Thoughts With Positivity

Most therapies and self-help strategies to help solve someone's overthinking will involve changing your overthinking tendencies into more positive thoughts. This change is necessary because positive thinking provides a person with numerous benefits. In this chapter, I will teach you about the benefits that positive thinking can bring into a person's life. By converting your overthinking into more positive thoughts, you will gain some of these benefits.

A person can increase their success using positive thinking.

Research studies have found that optimists tend to be more successful compared to pessimists. There was a research study that focused on the success of a few sales people. They found that the more optimistic salespeople made 88% more sales than the pessimistic salespeople. They found that optimistic salespeople were less likely to quit their jobs or give up during stressful work times. They were also more likely to describe a positive future when it came to their sales careers. This result makes a lot of sense. Having a more positive mindset at work prevents you from giving up and motivates you to work harder. It goes without saying that those who try harder than others and refusing to give up will be more successful than those that give up at the first hint of failure.

Social skills can be improved using positive thinking.

Having a better social life as an optimistic person is probably obvious at this point. People typically want to be around other positive people and often avoid those who are negative. Naturally, most people want to spend their time with optimistic people as they tend to be more cheerful and upbeat. They make better supporters and help encourage their friends to be better versions of themselves. Negative people tend to have a negative outlook on their own life, extending over to having a negative outlook on other people's lives. Generally, most people don't want to spend time with those who bring them down and makes them feel negative about their own life. Even negative people prefer to spend time with positive people. Having more positive thinking allows you to attract other positive thinkers to generate motivation and inspiration to achieve bigger and better things in life.

You can increase your ability to cope with stress using positive thinking.

Everybody deals with stress throughout their lives—some more than others. Especially if you are someone who overthinks a lot, you may feel more stress than others. However, everybody faces numerous stressful situations throughout their daily lives. This stress can come from financial stress, relationship problems, job stress, or stress from an illness. Although stress is a normal part of life, it is very important to manage it properly. High levels of stress can easily lead to depression and anxiety disorders. Researchers in the area of stress have found that more optimistic people are more likely to approach stressful situations by figuring out what actions they can take to manage it better. Rather than spending their time thinking negatively about the things that have gone wrong or using their energy, focusing on things that can't be changed, they focus on what they can change in the present moment. People with negative thinking usually take the opposite approach; they dwell on the fact that they cannot change their situation and create more negative thoughts. Optimistic people have more resilience when it comes to stress because they don't allow their minds to dwell on a negative situation. Instead, they look ahead and figure out how they can make their situation better.

Improving your mental health can be done through positive thinking.

Optimists are at a lower risk of experiencing mental health problems like anxiety and depression. In general, these people have better mental health compared to people who are pessimists. It remains true that we cannot simply cure people who suffer from depression/anxiety disorders by teaching them to think positively. Still, it does contribute to a healthier mind and more positive emotions over the long-term. When a person approaches their life with a positive outlook and perceives events more constructively, it is easier for them to deal with negative events that happen daily. If you are someone that doesn't see yourself as an optimist, you don't have to stress about it. Overcoming negative thought patterns isn't difficult, and you can do it to begin feeling the benefits of positive thinking. Later on, in this book, we will be learning how mindfulness can help you focus more on your thoughts in the present moment and not in the future and past. This practice can help ground someone to stop worrying about the future and focus on what's happening right now.

Positive thinking can greatly impact your physical health.

Typically, people who employ positive thinking have better mental health. Due to having better mental health, they are more likely to have better physical health as well. Optimistic people are also more likely to engage in healthy behaviors such as getting healthy amounts of sleep and exercise. Their ability to better cope with stress also lowers the amount of stress that their body is under. Researchers proved that optimists live longer, recover faster from illnesses/injuries, have stronger immune systems, are less likely to die from cardiovascular disease, and generally have better overall health. Since the mind and body are heavily connected, negative thinking contributes to lower physical health.

Chapter 4: How To Control Your Anxiety

Since overthinking and anxiety has a strong relationship, you must understand what anxiety is. In this chapter, you will get to learn about how you can reduce your anxiety levels. Reducing your anxiety levels will decrease the frequency of which you overthink. You will learn various techniques and therapies that you can try to reduce your anxiety to minimize your overthinking. Let's start with learning a little bit more about the science of anxiety.

Understanding The Science Behind Anxiety And Overthinking

Often, when people use the term' anxiety,' they are referring to generalized anxiety. Anxiety is a basic feeling and experience that all species of animals experience. Although anxiety is not a pleasant feeling, it is not dangerous. Anxiety is helpful for us in certain situations. Some people wish to get rid of anxiety completely, but that goal isn't possible or realistic!

We all have to keep in mind that anxiety is a normal emotion that is not dangerous. The symptoms of anxiety serve a function. Anxiety is a natural reaction to a perceived threat and helps us humans respond to it. However, if you have excessive anxiety, it can also be a problem.

Since anxiety is a normal response to a threat, when a person perceives that they are in a threatening situation, their fight or flight instinct is triggered. Its sole purpose is to protect itself by fighting or fleeing from danger. When somebody feels threatened, their brain sends messages to your autonomic nervous system (this is a section of your nerves). When this nervous system reacts, adrenalin and noradrenalin get released from your brain, which then triggers the anxiety response and automatically prepares us for danger. This nervous system eventually stops. It stops when our bodies destroy these chemicals in an attempt to calm the body down.

This fact is extremely important to remember because those who suffer from anxiety disorders feel like their anxiety will go on forever. However, biologically this cannot happen since anxiety is time-limited. Although it may feel that the anxiety is going on forever, it has a limited lifespan. After some time, your body will determine that it has had enough with the fight or flight instinct and restore the body to its neutral feeling. Anxiety cannot continue endlessly or damage your body. Although highly uncomfortable, this whole cycle is perfectly harmless and natural. This behavior is instinct to us because, in the wild, it is necessary for our bodies to reactive this response. After all, we know that danger can return.

Overall, the flight or flight response activates the entire body's metabolism. This response makes someone feel hot, flushed, and tired afterward because the entire process uses up a lot of energy.

After a strong anxiety experience, most people feel drained, tired, and completely washed out.

The action and process of worry are not the same as anxiety but plays a huge part in how anxiety happens or comes about. Worry is often the catalyst to a person's tendency to overthink. Overthinking begins when a person is worrying. This explanation means that to understand how overthinking works, we must understand how worry functions. In the simplest form, worry is involved with our thoughts, whereas anxiety is involved with our emotions. Worry and anxiety have a strong relationship, and when one is affected, the other one will be too. Depending on how intense your worry is, the transition from worry to anxiety can be longer or shorter. Anxiety is also very dependent on the situations you are worried about, and having too much worry can often lead to severe anxiety symptoms like panic and depression. When a person has excessive worry constantly, they are likely to suffer from a generalized anxiety disorder. According to psychologists in this field, they theorized that the action of worrying is often a misguided way for someone to avoid anxiety itself. Overthinking is the same concept; it is a misguided attempt for a person to avoid anxiety. This need is because you are attempting to prepare yourself for an anxiety-ridden situation if you are worrying and overthinking. By preparing, you attempt to make yourself feel better by creating possible solutions that can dissipate anxiety.

Worry has been a part of human life for a very long time. Many researchers in the field of anxiety constantly wonder if human ancestors worried just as much as we do now. Do they worry about whether or not they could hunt for food successfully? Or if the ancient farmers worried about whether or not their crops will have a good turn out? Unfortunately, we cannot prove this answer, but they likely did. Although we cannot document how far back worrying dates to, all signs point to the fact that ancient humans remembered yesterday and anticipated tomorrow just like us.

In our world today, there is plenty of documented evidence of worry. We even have phrases like "stop being such a worrywart!". Worry is so significant in our culture that an entire market of products aims to soothe nervous and anxious people. Products like stress relief soap or soothing teas are popular products in the self-help industry. Although worry dominates the Western world, many other cultures and people experience their worries and have developed their special ways of managing it. In the eastern part of our world, many people use tools like worry beads to relieve themselves of worry, nervousness, and anxiety. Worrywarts need to understand that they are not alone, and therefore, you don't need to deal with anxiety alone. A shocking 18% of the United States population are dealing with anxiety disorders, and 15% of the entire world worry excessively. 30% of the world worries minimally, and a shocking 55% worry somewhere between excessively and minimally. Every single person in this world has gone through the process of worry. A recent study concluded that 25% of people in the world today had met all the criteria for an anxiety disorder. That is an astounding statistic because it means that one in four people whom you know, likely are suffering from an anxiety disorder.

The process of worry is very subjective and can often be difficult to describe. The textbook definition of worry is 'a complex type of fear that feeds off the past and the future and spiral doubts and presumptions'. Other people who experience many bouts of worry a day describes it as:

- Worry is somewhere between concern and anxiety. The concern is the milder version of worry and anxiety is the stronger version of it. Anxiety is something you can feel physically, like an emotion, whereas worry is more of your head activity.
- Worry is the act and process of unproductive repetitive thinking.
- Worry can be acute or chronic. It can be likely to be about something where you have no control over or isn't realistic.

The feeling and the process of worry are usually described as; dominating, obsessive, preoccupying, frustrating, undesirable, tension inducing, negative, troublesome, and chronic. To help you understand the process of worry a little more, below are a few examples of worry that outlines how the process of worry causes people to overthink in different ways:

Example #1: "My girlfriend travels a lot due to her work. This travel is always something that worries me a lot. I often worry about the extreme things, to the point where I am constantly checking her flight status if they report a crash. I do this until she lands, and I hear that she's okay. I have gotten better over time, but I still do this every time she gets on a flight."

Example #2: "I caught a cold last week and ended up having to take two days off of work. The week before that happened, I avoided a situation at work because I was overwhelmed with other things that were much simpler to deal with. Due to my avoidance, it ended up escalating while I was not at work, and I think the situation would've turned out better if I had just dealt with it at the time. I was worried that my coworkers would be upset at me when I got back to work. I kept picturing the situation in my head and how I was going to approach that confrontation. When I did get back to the office, it appeared that nobody thought that it was a big deal. I was worried sick for absolutely no reason."

Example #3: "I am home renovation professional, and I am currently working with five different clients, and I worry about whether or not I can finish them all on time and to satisfaction. I start to wish that I would win the lottery to return the money to my client's so I don't have to finish the projects. However, I have never not completed a project before."

Example #4: "A lot of the times I would say something that I shouldn't have said, and I begin to replay that moment in my head numerous times and worry about it. When I see that person next, I will apologize for what I said, and they usually respond with "Don't worry about that!" or "What are you talking about?""

Example #5: "My grandfather is about to have heart surgery. The doctors told us that all signs point to it being a successful one, but there is the off chance that he may have a stroke during the surgery and not survive. The chances are very slim, but I can't help but worry about the worst-case scenario. I know worrying won't change anything, but I can't help it."

Example #6: "I was visiting my brother in New York City. My two daughters took a different flight from San Diego. They were supposed to land at 4 pm, and it's now 9 pm, and I still haven't heard from them. They have never been to NYC before, and I'm worried that they got lost because they don't know their way around. I was thinking about how they could've gotten into an accident on the way here, and I started worrying. I tried to stay calm, but I was sick to my stomach with worry. They ended up arriving safely."

These examples above showcase how worry affects different people in different triggering situations. If you experience something similar to this, try writing these worries down in a journal. You can see your feelings and thought process from an outside perspective by writing it out, which may help you take a step back and reprocess things.

You may be wondering if there are any benefits at all to the process of worrying. The answer is yes; there are many positive aspects to it. Most of the time, it is not easy to identify which aspects of worry you want to keep but keep in mind that they exist. Researchers use the analogy of worries being a signpost. You respect the nature and purpose of signposts, but you don't necessarily go out of your way to find them. These signposts have a purpose, and you should try to use them for good, but once it served its purpose, you don't need to look for them anymore. Worry is an adaptive process; instead of having it work against you, you should control it so that it works for you.

Symptoms Of Anxiety And Overthinking

Sometimes, people who suffer from anxiety might not even know that that's the cause. They may simply feel as if their overthinking makes them feel sick but don't realize that it is the anxiety that is the cause of their physical ailments. Since many anxiety symptoms are very physical, most people may think they have a medical condition. Often, these symptoms can be managed or tamed using simple over the counter drugs, but sometimes you have to get to the root cause to help alleviate it. When anxiety becomes larger than the situations that triggered them, they begin to interfere with your life. This situation could then lead to an anxiety disorder. By recognizing the anxiety symptoms, you can figure out how to get the help you need.

Below are all the most common symptoms of anxiety. Each symptom will be explained in more detail to get you a comprehensive understanding of it.

- Excessive Worrying And Overthinking

As we just discussed, worrying is the most common 'symptom' of anxiety. However, we often see worry as the cause of anxiety, which then produces more worry. It's a vicious cycle. When worrying is associated with anxiety disorders, the amount and intensity of worry are usually disproportionate to the situations that triggered it. It often occurs in normal daily situations. For an individual to be officially diagnosed with anxiety, worrying has to occur almost every day for a minimum of six months with difficulty in controlling it.

Moreover, worrying has to be at a severe level, making it hard for people to concentrate and complete their daily routine. It doesn't mean that if you experience worry every often, it means you have an anxiety disorder. Statistics state that people under the age of 65 are at a higher risk of anxiety disorders, especially those in lower socioeconomic status, and have more life stressors.

- Excessive Agitation

Biologically, when somebody is feeling anxious, their nervous system begins to go into overdrive. This overaction of the nervous system kicks off a series of effects throughout the human body. Symptoms of agitation can include a racing heart, shaky hands, dry mouth, and sweaty palms. When your brain senses danger, it begins to prepare your body to react to the danger, which leads to the symptoms above. Your body begins to relocate blood away from your digestive system and to your muscles instead, in case you need to fight or run. Your senses become heightened, and your heart rate increases. Although this is extremely helpful in the presence of a real threat, it is debilitating if the fear is just in your head.

- Restlessness

Another common symptom of anxiety is restlessness; this is primarily dominant in teenagers and children. The feeling of restlessness feels like; having an uncomfortable urge always to move or feel 'on edge'. This feeling showcases itself in the form of tapping your fingers or your leg repeatedly. A recent study of children diagnosed with anxiety found that over 70% suffered from restlessness as their main symptom of anxiety. Although restlessness is not a symptom in everybody who experiences anxiety, it is one of the first major symptoms doctors look for when making a diagnosis.

- Fatigue

Another common symptom of an anxiety disorder is the tendency to become easily fatigued. This fatigue can be surprising to most people as anxiety is often associated with symptoms such as restlessness or hyperactivity. In this case, Fatigue can be either chronic or following a panic attack depending on the individual. It is not very clear whether fatigue is a symptom due to anxiety itself or a symptom of insomnia or muscle tension, which are also symptoms of anxiety. It could also be due to the hormonal effects caused by chronic anxiety. Keep in mind that fatigue is also a symptom of other medical conditions or depression. Just feeling tired alone is not enough evidence to diagnose an anxiety disorder.

- Concentration Difficulty

Many people who suffer from anxiety addresses their concentration difficulty. A recent study of teenagers and children suffering from GAD (Generalized Anxiety Disorder) came back with results showing that more than two-thirds of this demographic had difficulty concentrating. Also, the same study but with adults found that 90% of them had difficulty concentration. They identified that the worse their anxiety was, the more difficulty they had. Scientific studies have found that anxiety can interrupt working memory. This kind of memory is the one we use to hold out short-term information. Due to this evidence, it explains why people's performance decreases dramatically during periods of high anxiety. Since the brain's short-term memory function is also affected, people also report struggling to remember things during an anxiety-ridden situation. Keep in mind, just like some other symptoms, that difficulty concentration could be a symptom of other medical conditions. This concentration problem is also a symptom of attention deficit disorder and depression.

This symptom on its own does not indicate that you have anxiety.

- Irritability

Anxious people often experience excessive irritability. This irritability is often in the form of having low patience levels and having angry outbursts. Small daily things can easily set an anxious person off when they are suffering the symptoms of irritation. In a recent study of over 6000 adults, over 90% of these people suffering from GAD reported that they were highly irritable during bouts of extreme anxiety. Compared to teenagers and children, young and middle-aged adults diagnosed with GAD were proven to be two times as irritable in their daily lives. This symptom makes a lot of sense, given that anxiety is associated with excessive worrying and high arousal.

- Tense Muscles

Having tense muscles more often than not, is a common symptom of anxiety. We do not yet fully understand why tense muscles are such a common symptom of anxiety. It could have something to do with our brain sending extra blood to our muscles when the fight or flight response is activated. If this happens a lot, your muscles may become overtired and, therefore, tense. It is also possible that muscle tenseness itself increases anxiety due to the uncomfortable physical feeling.

On the contrary, it could also be the other way around where anxiety increases muscle tenseness. Muscle relaxation therapy is proven to reduce the worry of people with GAD. Some studies even indicate that muscle relaxation therapy is as effective as Cognitive Behavioral Therapy (CBT), which is known as the best therapy for anxiety.

- Insomnia

Sleep disturbances, such as trouble falling asleep or staying asleep, are strongly associated with anxiety disorders. One of the two most commonly reported problems is waking up in the middle of the night or having trouble falling asleep. This sleep disturbance is likely due to the worrying and spiraled thinking in an anxious person's head. Often, they don't even realize that they got caught up in their thoughts, and without being able to shut that off, their body won't be able to relax enough to fall asleep. Research suggests that often, those who had insomnia during childhood develop anxiety in their adulthood. A similar study followed almost 1000 children over 20 years; they found that children who had insomnia during their childhood had a 60% increased risk of developing an anxiety order by their mid-20s. Similar to the symptoms above, it is unclear whether insomnia contributes to anxiety or if anxiety contributes to insomnia. However, doctors proved that once you properly treat an anxiety disorder, insomnia often improves along with it. This improvement is due to the strong relationship between anxiety and insomnia.

- Panic Attacks

We will be diving into more detail regarding panic attacks in the next chapter, but panic attacks or anxiety attacks are commonly associated with anxiety. Panic attacks are their form of an anxiety disorder; this is called "Panic Disorder." Simply put, panic attacks are when an individual feels an overwhelming, intense sensation of fear that can be completely debilitating. This fear comes with the symptoms of a racing heart, shakiness, sweating, fear of dying, chest tightness, and shortness of breath. Panic attacks can happen in public places or if you are by yourself. If an individual finds that they have panic attacks frequently and unexpectedly, the likely are suffering from a panic disorder. A shocking statistic of 22% of adults in the population has experienced panic attacks at some point in their life. However, only 3% meet the criteria for a panic disorder.

- Avoidance Of Certain Situations

One of the more common anxiety disorders that lead to avoidance of situations is a social anxiety disorder. Individuals exhibiting signs of this disorder typically feel:

- Anxious or scared regarding upcoming social situations or gatherings
- Worried that others are judging them
- Scared of being humiliated or embarrassed in front of people

- Avoiding certain social gatherings or events due to these fears

Social anxiety is one of the more common anxiety disorders and affects about 12% of the American population. This type of disorder usually begins to develop in early life. 50% of people who suffer from social anxiety got diagnosed by the age of 11, and 80% are diagnosed by age 20. Often, those who suffer from social anxiety appear very shy and quiet when meeting new people or in a group activity. They may not appear distressed on the outside, but they are extremely fearful and anxious on the inside. Often, this aloofness can cause people with social anxiety to appear ditzy, snobby, or standoffish. Still, it is often associated with other things like depression, low self-esteem, and high self-criticism.

- Irrational Fears

Irrational fears are a symptom of anxiety, specific to phobia disorders. A phobia disorder is when an individual has extreme fears about specific things like heights, enclosed spaces, or spiders. This fear is often severe enough that it interferes with your ability to live your daily life or even function properly.

- Weight Loss/Gain

Many people facing anxiety disorders often report that they have had significant weight loss or weight gain. Whether it's a loss or a gain varies from person to person. Often, anxiety leads to missing meals or bad food choices. It could also lead to completely losing the desire to eat. We have often seen that a common symptom of anxiety is indigestion or irritable bowel syndrome. Often, when you are anxious, and your fight or flight response is activated, it speeds up your metabolism, using more of your energy. If somebody is not properly eating and their metabolism is often on high, then it is likely that they will lose weight.

Similarly, anxiety contributes to weight gain because hormonal levels get mixed up during the presence of extreme anxiety. This hormone change results in a fat buildup in the stomach and leads to an increase in weight. You may often notice that when someone has gained weight due to anxiety, the excess weight comes on in the stomach area.

- Compulsive Behavior

A not as common anxiety disorder is Obsessive-Compulsive Disorder (OCD). A lot of times, anxious people become faced with compulsive habits. If these habits become debilitating and prevent you from living your normal life, it likely becomes OCD. OCD is when you have recurring and obsessive thoughts of checking certain things over and over to make sure it is safe. Many people who suffer from OCD tend to feel extreme shame about their need to carry out their compulsive actions. These feelings of shame and secrecy tend to be the leading cause of delayed diagnosis and treatment.

OCD is not as common as other anxiety disorders and symptoms but is one that we can easily treat if you or your doctors catch it early on. Only about 3% of the population have experienced OCD in their lifetime. People can experience OCD as early as six years old, but symptoms don't fully develop until adolescence.

- Addictions

Although it is arguable whether addiction is a symptom of anxiety or anxiety causes addictions, anxious people are more likely to become addicted to substances like alcohol, cigarettes, or drugs. Often, it is less to do with the 'want' behind using these substances but more of the 'need'. Anxious people tend to turn to illicit substances to self-medicate other symptoms of anxiety. For example, a person suffering from social anxiety disorder may turn to alcohol during social gatherings to relieve some of the stress and anxiety that comes with having to socialize. Often, they may become reliant on alcohol to help them cope with situations that they are uncomfortable with. If they have many normal daily situations in life that they are uncomfortable with, they begin to drink more often than not, leading to alcohol addiction.

Some of the symptoms that we have discussed in this chapter are arguably the conditions of their own. Social anxiety disorder, panic disorder, and OCD can all be classified as an individual anxiety disorder while also being a symptom of general anxiety. In the later chapters of this book, we will take a deeper look at these anxiety disorders and their specific symptoms.

Remember that to be diagnosed with an anxiety disorder, you must show multiple symptoms for a minimum of 6 months or more. This rule for diagnosis means that if you only showcase one symptom, like weight loss, it does not mean that you have an anxiety disorder. It means that your weight loss symptoms could be because of something else like a lifestyle change or a medical condition.

Anxiety Management Techniques That Reduces Overthinking

Since anxiety connects so deeply to overthinking, relieving anxiety can help decrease the amount that you overthink. We use numerous methods to relieve anxiety; this includes speaking therapies like Cognitive Behavioral Therapy, medication, meditation, and other self-help methods. In this chapter, we will look at the most common and effective methods of relieving anxiety.

Cognitive Behavioral Therapy (CBT)

Cognitive Behavioral Therapy has been an increasingly hot topic in psychology in the past few years. More and more therapists and psychiatrists adapt to this type of speaking therapy due to its proven effectiveness in treating common mental disorders like anxiety and depression. Although we hear about this term a lot, what exactly is it? Cognitive Behavioral Therapy is rooted in the theory that a person's thoughts (cognition), emotion, and behavior are all constantly interacting with one another; therefore, if one of these three components are affected, the rest will be affected as well. Cognition is responsible for how we think and what we think, emotion is responsible for how we feel, and behavior is responsible for how we act. These three components all support the theory that if a person merely changes their thoughts or the way they think, it will impact our feelings, which will ultimately determine our behavior. In simple terms, this means that people who may be having negative or unrealistic thoughts that cause them distress could result in behavioral problems. When a person is suffering from psychological distress, the way they perceive certain situations can become contorted, this could cause negative behaviors.

In today's society, Cognitive Behavioral Therapy is used to treat mental disorders, primarily anxiety and depression. Due to its long history and development, CBT is a practical and time-saving form of psychotherapy. CBT focuses on your here-and-now problems that come up in daily life. People use it to help people make sense of their surroundings and events that happen around them. CBT is very structured, time-saving, and problem-focused. These advantages are why CBT is one of the most popular techniques when used to deal with mental disorders in our fast-paced modern lives.

In the present day, CBT works by helping clients recognize, question, and change the thoughts that relate to the emotional and behavioral reactions that cause them difficulty. By using CBT to monitor and record thoughts during undesirable situations, people begin to learn that the way they think contributes to their emotional problems. Modern-day Cognitive Behavioral Therapy helps reduce emotional problems by teaching individuals to:

- Identify any distortions in their thinking process
- See their thoughts as ideas rather than facts
- Take a step back from their thoughts to look at situations from another perspective

The new CBT model used in the present day focuses on the relationship between thoughts and behaviors. Both can influence each other. There are three levels and types of thoughts:

- Conscious thoughts: These are rational thoughts that happen with complete awareness
- Automatic thoughts: These are the thoughts that move very quickly; you are likely not to be fully aware of their movement. These thoughts mean that it's difficult to check them for accuracy. A person suffering from mental health problems may have thoughts that are entirely not logical.
- Schemas: These are the core beliefs and personal values when it comes to processing information. Our childhood and other life experiences shape our Schemas.

Although Cognitive Behavioral Therapy is currently the most common speaking therapy that treats overthinking and anxiety, other therapies can do the same job. The concept behind these other therapies is to help resolve any internal problems that the victim may be suffering from. Focusing on this helps them feel more confident in themselves, thus lowering the amount they overthink. In this subchapter, we will look at two other speaking therapies; interpersonal therapy and psychodynamic therapy.

Interpersonal Therapy (IPT)

Interpersonal psychotherapy (IPT) is a focused, evidence-based, and time-limited approach to treat mood disorders. Improving the quality of a person's interpersonal relationships and social functioning to reduce their distress is the main goal of IPT. IPT helps provide the client with strategies to resolve problems within four main areas:

1. It focuses on addressing interpersonal deficits, such as involvement in unfulfilling relationships and social isolation.
2. IPT helps clients manage unresolved grief, especially if the reason for their distress is linked to the loss of a loved one either in the past or recently.
3. IPT can also help with difficult life transitions, such as moving to another city, divorce, or retirement.
4. Doctors also recommend IPT for people that face interpersonal conflicts that emerge from

family members, coworkers, partners, or close friends.

Improvement in these areas helps prevent overthinking as the person will feel more satisfied in their day-to-day life, limiting the reasons that cause overthinking.

IPT was originally developed to treat major depressive disorders. It is also effectively used to treat perinatal depression, eating disorders, drug, and alcohol abuse, dysthymia, and other mood disorders such as bipolar disorder (BPD). IPT is different from traditional therapy types by focusing on the present rather than past relationships or upbringing. This practice is different from CBT because it addresses maladaptive thoughts and behaviors only concerning how they affect interpersonal relationships. IPT's goal is to change the relationship patterns rather than the depressive symptoms and target relationship struggles that exacerbate the symptoms. IPT is less structured than CBT as it focuses on the areas that the client has specified without focusing on their personality traits.

Treatment using IPT usually happens in using individual therapy sessions and group work. IPT lasts between 12 and 16 weeks. Its treatment is daily structured and includes continuous assessment, interviews from the therapist, and homework. The first phase of IPT requires the therapist to assess the client's social history and depressive symptoms within the first three sessions. They examine the client's social history in-depth, noting any changes in their relationship patterns and changes. Then, the therapist will work with the client to implement treatment strategies specific to their problem areas. As treatment progresses, they may change their targeted problem area. Group sessions are similar to the individual ones because they are semi-structured, focused on interpersonal dynamics, and are time-limited. Group therapies provide clients a safe and supportive environment to practice their interpersonal skills. Group therapy also includes pre-treatment, mid-treatment, and post-treatment meetings to review the client's individual progress, goals, and strategies.

IPT has developed over 20 years ago and was originally supposed to be a time-structured treatment for severe depression people. In recent years, it gained a lot of popularity. IPT practitioners believe that changing a person's social environment is an important factor in treating depression and preventing it. IPT was originally developed for adults, but it has been modified in recent years, so adolescents and older adults can benefit from it.

Psychodynamic Therapy

Psychodynamic therapy is similar to psychoanalytic therapy in a way that is an in-depth form of talking therapy based on psychoanalysis principles and theories. However, psychodynamic therapy is not as focused on the relationship between the client and therapist but focuses on the client's relationship with their external world. Usually, psychodynamic therapy does not last as long as psychoanalytic therapy when it comes to the number of sessions and the frequency of sessions. However, this differs case by case.

Psychodynamic therapy focused on treating depression and other severe psychological disorders. It focuses especially on the people who may have lost meaning in their lives and struggle to maintain and form personal relationships. By recovering those areas in a person's life, they spend less time dwelling and overthinking their problems. Studies have found that people who suffer from eating disorders, addiction, and social anxiety disorders benefit from psychodynamic therapy. During psychodynamic therapy, the client is encouraged to speak about anything that comes to mind, including dreams, desires, fantasies, current issues, and the therapist's help. This therapy aims to reduce their depression systems and achieve other benefits such as better use of their abilities and talents, increasing self-esteem, and an improved ability to develop and maintain better relationships. The client may continue to experience the benefits even after this therapy has ended. Some patients may find that short-term therapy (less than one year) is sufficient; some other patients may require long-term therapy to gain lasting effects.

Psychodynamic therapy's theories and techniques distinguish it from other forms of therapy by helping them acknowledge, recognize, express, understand, and overcome contradictory and negative feelings. This type of therapy also helps you acknowledge repressed emotions and improve their interpersonal relationships and experiences. This work includes helping the client understand how their previous repressed emotions affect their current behavior, relationships, and decision-making. This type of therapy also aims to help the client who may be aware of their social difficulties but don't have the tools or skills to overcome this problem by themselves. During this therapy, the clients will learn to analyze and resolve their current issues and then change their behavior in their current relationships by using deep exploration and analysis of their past experiences and emotions.

Medication

If your overthinking happens because of a mental disorder like anxiety or depression, then taking medication may improve your condition. However, if your overthinking isn't a symptom of a mental disorder, you may not want to take medication. Simple practices of self-esteem, self-discipline, and therapy may be enough to lower the amount that you overthink. However, it is still beneficial to understand how medications work to balance the chemicals in your brain. Many people with mental disorders find that medication helps them control their brains from overthinking and spiraling. The most common form of medication for mental disorders is antidepressants.

Antidepressants are supposed to adjust the neurotransmitters in the brain to help correct the balance of chemicals. When a person is in the trenches of suffering from the pain and anguish of depression, simply taking a pill can sound like a convenient and simple relief method. However, it is important to keep in mind that depression isn't only a result of an imbalance in brain chemicals. Instead, it is a combination of that and other psychological, biological, and social factors that include coping skills, relationships, and lifestyle, all of which medication would not address. However, this doesn't mean that antidepressants don't work. When a person's depression is severe, medication can be very helpful and even lifesaving. Although it can help relieve symptoms for some people, antidepressants do not cure depression and are not supposed to be long-term solutions. As more time passes, people who initially found antidepressants to be useful can slip back into depression; this goes the same for the people who stop taking the medication. Also, antidepressants sometimes come with undesirable side effects, so people need to consider the pros and cons of taking depression medication.

People who have mild to moderate depression find that exercise, self-help strategies, and therapy works just as well, or even better than medication. It also doesn't come with any side effects. As we mentioned earlier in this chapter, even if you decide to take antidepressants, it is also important to pursue other changes in your life to address whatever the underlying issue may be and overcome your overthinking for good.

Chapter 5: How To Manage Your Unhelpful Thoughts

In this chapter, we will learn some more ways to manage your unhelpful thoughts. First, I will outline some of the most common thinking patterns present in the minds of people who tend to overthink. Then, I will share with you some strategies for overcoming these thought patterns. This chapter will set you up for success going forward!

An essential aspect of getting your overthinking control is gaining the ability to control what thoughts linger in your mind. There are numerous ways to accomplish this. Cognitive Behavioral Therapy is one of these ways, as it can help you identify which thoughts in your mind are evidence-based and which aren't. We have already looked at Cognitive Behavioral Therapy and how it can help you with this, and in this chapter, we will look at some new strategies. Next, we will explore mindfulness meditation as being mindful can help you pay more attention to the present moment. This mindfulness will also prevent overthinking. Lastly, we will be looking at how improving your physical health can help you overcome negativity in your life, which will reduce the number of negative thoughts that come about through overthinking. Without further ado, let's begin!

Unhelpful Thought Patterns

To effectively manage your thoughts and reduce overthinking, you must understand the different types of 'unhealthy thinking patterns' present in people who overthink. By identifying these unhealthy thinking styles, you can change your thoughts from unhealthy ones into healthier and more positive thoughts. Thus, this will lower the amount that you overthink.

Knowing what these different unhelpful thinking styles are, you can begin to identify when using them. When you notice your mind using them, you will learn how to use CBT techniques to change those thoughts/worries into helpful ones. By determining whether your worries are justified or not, you can control those worries. You can then prevent these worries from causing you anxiety, which then causes overthinking.

Below are the twelve most common types of unhealthy thinking patterns exhibited by individuals who suffer from overthinking problems.

All at once, bias: This is when you think risks and threats are right at your front door, and the amount of it is increasing as well. When this occurs, you tend to:

a. Think that negative situations are evolving quicker than you can come up with solutions
b. Think that situations are moving so quickly that you feel overwhelmed

c. Think that there is no time between now and the impending threat
d. Numerous risks and threats seem to all appear at the same time

Jumping to conclusions: You make a negative assumption even when you don't have supporting evidence. There are two types of jumping to conclusions:

a. Mind reading: You imagine that you already know what other people are thinking negatively of you, and therefore you don't bother to ask.
b. Fortune-telling: You predict that things will end up badly, and you convince yourself that your prediction is a fact.

Overgeneralization: You see one single negative situation as a pattern that never ends. You draw conclusions of future situations based on one single event.

All or nothing thinking: This is otherwise known as 'black and white thinking.' You tend to see things in either black or white or success or failure. If your performance is not perfect, you will see it as a failure.

Disqualifying the positive: You discount your positive experiences or success by saying, "that doesn't count." By discounting all your positive experiences, you can maintain a negative perspective even if your actions contradict this perspective daily.

Magnification/Minimization: You blow things out of proportion or inappropriately shrink something to make it seem unimportant. For example, you beef up somebody else's achievement (magnification) and shrug off your own (minimization).

Emotional reasoning: You assume that your negative emotions reflect the reality. For example, "I feel it so, therefore, it is true."

Catastrophizing: You associate terrible and extreme consequences to the outcome of situations and events. For example, if someone rejects you when you ask them on a date, you tell yourself that it means you will be alone forever. Another example would be when you make an error at work and assume that you will get fired.

Labeling and mislabeling: This is overgeneralization to the extreme. Instead of describing your mistake, you automatically associate a negative label to yourself: "I'm a loser."

You also do this to others when someone else's behavior is undesirable. For example, you attach "they are a loser" to them as well.

Personalization: You take responsibility for something that wasn't your fault. You see yourself as the cause of an external situation.

Mental filter: You choose one single undesirable detail, and you exclusively dwell on it. Your perception of reality becomes negative based on this detail., making it a filter over your life. You only notice your failures, but you don't look at your successes.

"Should" statements: You motivate yourself using the words "should" and "shouldn't" as if you associate a reward or punishment to certain things before taking any action. Since you associate a reward or a punishment for yourself with these words, you feel anger or frustration when other people don't follow this scheme for life.

By understanding these unhealthy thinking patterns, you will begin to notice them happening in your mind. When you notice these unhelpful thinking patterns, you can learn to interrupt them while they are in process and say, for example, "I'm catastrophizing again." When you can interrupt your unhelpful thinking styles, you can readjust it to something more helpful. In the next section, we will be discussing some tips and tricks to help you challenge your unhealthy thinking patterns. This strategy is one of the main ones used in CBT.

Challenging Your Unhealthy Thinking Patterns

Once you can identify your unhelpful thinking styles, you can begin trying to reshape those thoughts into something more realistic and factual. In this chapter, I have categorized all the different cognitive distortions and what questions you should be asking yourself to develop different thoughts.

Keep in mind that it takes a lot of effort and dedication to change our thoughts, so don't get frustrated if you do not succeed right away. You probably have had these thoughts for a while, so don't expect it to change overnight.

Probability Overestimation

If you find that you have thoughts about a possible negative outcome, but you are noticing that you often overestimate the probability, try asking yourself the questions below to reevaluate your thoughts.
- Based on my experience, what is the probability that this thought will come true realistically?
- What are the other possible results from this situation? Is the outcome that I am thinking of now the only possible one? Does my feared outcome have the highest possible chance of occurring when compared to the other outcomes?
- Have I ever experienced this type of situation before? If so, what happened? What have I learned from these past experiences that would be helpful to me now?
- If a friend or loved one is having these thoughts, what would I say to them?

Catastrophizing

- If the prediction that I am afraid of really did come true, how bad would it be?
- If I am feeling embarrassed, how long will this last? How long will other people remember/talk about it? What are some examples of the different things they could be saying? Am I 100% certain that they will only have bad things to say?
- I am feeling uncomfortable right now, but is this a horrible or unbearable outcome?
- What are the other alternatives for how this situation could turn out?
- If a friend or loved one was having these thoughts, what would I say to them?

Mind Reading
- Is it possible that I know what other people's thoughts are? What are the other things they could be thinking about?
- Do I have any evidence to support my assumptions?
- In the scenario that my assumption is true, what is so bad about it?

Personalization
- What other elements might be playing a role in the situation? Could it be the other person's stress, deadlines, or mood?
- Does somebody always have to be at blame?
- A conversation is never just one person's responsibility.
- Were any of these circumstances out of my control?

Should Statements
- Would I be holding the same standards to a loved one or a friend?
- Are there any exceptions?
- Would someone else do this differently?

All or Nothing Thinking
- Is there a middle ground or a grey area that I am not considering?
- Would I judge a friend or loved one in the same way?
- Was the entire situation 100% negative? Was there any part of the situation that I handled well?
- Is having/showing some anxiety such a horrible thing?

Selective Attention/Memory
- What are the positive elements of the situation? Am I ignoring those?
- Would a different person see this situation differently?
- What strengths do I have? Am I ignoring those?

Negative Core Beliefs
- Do I have any evidence that supports my negative beliefs?
- Is this thought true in every situation?
- Would a loved one or friend agree with my self-belief?

Once you catch yourself using these unhelpful thinking patterns, ask yourself the above questions to begin changing your thoughts. Remember, CBT's core basis is that your thoughts affect your emotions, which then influences your behavior (overthinking). By catching and changing your thoughts before it spirals, you will be in control of your emotions and behavior as well.

Using Mindfulness Meditation To Control Your Thoughts

Mindfulness is also an element in Cognitive Behavioral Therapy, but you can also use it independently by performing meditation. So what exactly is mindfulness or meditation? Mindfulness is a type of meditation used as a mental training practice that requires you to focus your mind on your thoughts and sensations in the present moment. Your thoughts include your physical sensations, passing thoughts, and current emotions.

Mindfulness Meditation often utilizes mental imagery, breathing practice, muscle and body relaxation, and awareness of your mind and body. For beginners, I recommend that you follow a guided meditation to direct them through the entire process. If nobody is guiding you through this meditation, it is easy to drift away and fall asleep. That is not the purpose of meditation. When you become more skilled in doing mindfulness meditation, you will be able to do it without a guide or any vocal guidance.

The most original and standardized mindfulness meditation program is called the Mindfulness-Based Stress Reduction (MSBR) program. This meditation was developed by a Ph.D. student who was a student of a famous Buddhist monk. This program focuses on helping individuals bring their awareness to the present and focus on their awareness. This meditation has increased in popularity and is not incorporated into medical settings to treat health conditions such as anxiety, insomnia, pain, and stress. Although this meditation is quite straightforward, professionals recommend finding a teacher or a program that can act as a guide when you begin. I recommend that most people do this meditation for at least 10 minutes per day. If you don't have a lot of free time, that's okay. Even just a few minutes a day plays a huge role in changing your wellbeing. Follow these instructions below to get started:

1. Find a place that is quiet and that you feel comfortable in. Ideally, this is your home or a place where you feel safe. Sit in something comfortable like a chair and make sure your head and back are straight and aligned. Try to release any tension you feel.
2. Begin to sort your thoughts and put away the ones that are of the past or future. Focus on your thoughts that are about the present.
3. Begin to bring your awareness to your breath. Focus on the sensation of air moving through

your body when you inhale and exhale. Focus on this feeling. Begin to feel the movement of your belly as it rises and falls. Feel how the air enters through your nostrils and leaves through your mouth. Pay attention to how each breath is different.
4. Watch your thoughts come and go in front of you. Pretend you are watching the clouds, letting them slowly pass before you. It doesn't matter if your thought is a worry, anxiety, hope, or fear - when these thoughts pass by, don't ignore them or suppress them. Simply just acknowledge them calmly and anchor yourself by focusing on your breathing.
5. If you find yourself being carried away by your thoughts, observe where your mind drifted off to and without judging yourself, simply anchor yourself by focusing on your breathing. Getting carried away happens a lot with beginners, so don't be hard on yourself if you drift away. Always use your breathing as an anchor.
6. When you are nearing the final two minutes of your session, sit still for those two minutes, and bring awareness to your physical location. Get up slowly.

Incorporating Mindfulness Into Your Life

Mindfulness meditation is the simplest technique in the meditation field. However, there are other ways of practicing mindfulness that isn't only in the form of meditation. There are a few opportunities in your day where you can use to practice mindfulness. Here are a few suggestions of when you may have the time to practice mindfulness:

1. **Doing the dishes:** This is a wonderful window of time where you can use to practice mindfulness. Typically, when you are doing the dishes, there isn't anyone trying to get your attention. This act is a perfect time to try mindfulness. Try focusing on the sensation of warm water on your hands, the look and feel of bubbles, the smell of your dish soap, and your plates' sounds clunking in the water. Try to give yourself to this experience and feel your mind refreshing and your anxiety fading.
2. **Brushing your teeth:** Since you have to brush your teeth every day, you can use this time frame to practice mindfulness. Start by feeling your weight on your feet against the floor, your toothbrush's feeling in the hand, and the movement as you begin to brush your teeth. Focus on these feelings and the thoughts you are having in the present. Don't dwell; just acknowledge those thoughts as they come and go.
3. **Driving:** This is one of those activities where it's easy for people to do mindlessly. Mindlessness is more likely to happen if you are driving the same route every day. Make use of this time by not letting your mind wander off to think about what you need to do that day. Practice mindfulness by trying to keep yourself

anchored. Notice all sensations and visuals, like the colors you see, the smell of your car, and the steering wheel's feeling. Focus your attention on all of the sounds and noises you hear. If you find yourself wandering, bring your attention back to where you are in your car.
4. **Exercising:** Make your workout routine a time also to exercise mindfulness. Try to exercise away from screens or music and focus only on your breathing and moving your feet. Although watching TV or listening to music will make your workout go by faster or distract you from any anxiety, it won't help manage unhealthy thoughts. Bring your attention to feeling how your muscles feel and pay attention to how your body reacts to your workout. Instead of ignoring the pains you may be feeling, acknowledge it, and let yourself feel the exercise.
5. **Bedtime:** This is normally the time where you begin to get things ready for the next day. Instead of battling too much with it, just keep in mind what you need to do. Stop trying to rush through it to get to bed but try to enjoy the experience of completing those actual tasks. Focus on what you need to do and don't think about what is next. Start early to leave yourself with enough time so you don't need to rush through things. Any thoughts or anxieties that come up should be acknowledged and let go.

Mindfulness Meditation Example Script

To help you even further control your anxiety, worry, and overthinking, I will provide you with a meditation transcript that you can follow to relax your mind. The biggest benefit of this meditation is when you perform it at a time of anxiety or stress. It will help guide you into a relaxed state where you can refocus your attention on the present. This meditation is useful when you find that your mind is racing, and you can also use it when you feel like you are on the verge of a panic attack. We call this meditation "the Joyful Mind Meditation." Below, you will see an example script for this meditation.

Welcome to the Joyful Mind guided meditation.

Please find a quiet area to sit and dim the lighting.

Sit back with your shoulders relaxed and straight. Loosen any clothing that may be restricting you and make sure you are comfortable.

Rest your hands loosely on your lap and close your eyes. Take a deep breath. Relax.

Now that you have closed your eyes, you may begin to connect with your inner self on your thoughts and feelings.

Gradually, allow the outside world to fade away from your awareness.

Over the next few minutes, allow yourself to enjoy this relaxing experience and submerge yourself into it.

During this meditation, you do not need to think of any of your responsibilities. Any tasks, thoughts, or concerns do not require any immediate attention. Tuck those thoughts aside and focus on your inner thoughts.

You may find your mind to be wandering during this meditation. Mind-wandering is fine and is normal. Simply just bring your awareness back to the present and the sound of this meditation. I will guide you to a place of deep relaxation and inner peace.

Remember that you are the one in control. If you want to end this meditation, do so by simply opening your eyes.

Begin to take a breath, slow, long, and deep through your nose. Release that breath through your mouth.

Feel that your inner self is beginning to relax.

Begin to inhale another deep breath, then exhale.

Pay attention to how calming this type of breathing is. Bring your awareness to the feelings of relaxation throughout your body. Focus on how it feels from your lungs to your toes.

Continue to breathe slowly, deeply, and gently. Try not to breathe too fast.

With each breath you take, your thoughts begin to feel lighter.

You may start to feel a sense of spaciousness inside of you. It will begin to open up more.

Keep relaxing.

Allow the gentle movement of your inhale and exhale to guide you to a more relaxed state.

Inhale, exhale. You will begin to go deeper into this state of relaxation.

Breathe in, and breathe out. Allow your mind to slow down gradually. Inhale, exhale. Let's begin to slow it down even more.

Inhale, and exhale.

You are now in a complete state of relaxation. You can now begin to enjoy this guided journey to find your inner place of joy and serenity.

Allow yourself to have imagery and visualizations as I speak. Do this at your own pace.

If you are having trouble visualizing mental imagery, try sensing those surroundings instead of picturing them.

Start to let your expectations drift away. Let them go and allow yourself to feel this journey in the form that comes naturally to you.

Start to imagine a grassy, green, and beautiful field. You are standing in it. The field goes on for miles. You can feel the sun's heat shining on your face, slowly bringing warmth to your whole body.

You feel the lushness and softness of the grass that is cushioning your feet. The smell of nature engulfs you.

You hear the many sounds of nature in your surroundings. In the distance, you hear the rustling of blowing grass and trees. The birds are singing.

You feel very at home in this place.

You have all the time in the world.

You are safe and happy here.

Take a moment to enjoy and appreciate your surroundings.

You notice a large beautiful tree growing nearby.

You begin to walk towards the tree.

Take your time walking to this tree. Stay in the moment and appreciate how each step feels. There is no rush to get to this tree.

As you walk towards the tree, you begin to feel yourself falling into a deeper state of relaxation.

You are now standing under the tree. It's branches and leaves hang above your head.

You notice that this treat bears many fruits in all different shapes, colors, and sizes.

This tree isn't an ordinary tree. Its fruit harbors special powers.

Reach your arm up to the branches and take a piece of fruit. Look at the fruit for a moment. Pay attention to the color, texture, and weight of this fruit. It feels quite heavy.

Take a bite of this fruit.

As you swallow a bite of the fruit, it slides down your throat and into your belly. You begin to feel something wonderful.

A feeling of happiness and peacefulness begins to grow inside of you.

This happiness and peacefulness grow from your stomach and are spreading to your chest and into your heart.

Let go of all thinking and bring your awareness to the feeling. Embellish the sensation of peace, love, and joy. Feel your body glow with these feelings.

Take another bite of this special fruit and savor it. Let yourself taste it.

This wonderful feeling intensifies.

Feel your body begin to radiate this sensation of love and happiness. It feels beautiful.

Take another bite of the fruit, and let yourself take as many bites as you want.

Relax and allow yourself to drown in this enchantment. Don't try and just let it take over your body effortlessly. Break down any walls that you are comfortable breaking and let it surround you.

Stay with these feelings of joy and peace. Enjoy this time of meditation.

You can choose to remain in this relaxed state for as long as you want, don't feel rushed to leave.

When you are ready, you can end this meditation. Simply open your eyes to leave the meditation. Take a few deep breaths and give yourself some time to adjust before standing up.

Incorporating Healthier Lifestyle Changes

Lifestyle changes may be seemingly simple, but they are very powerful tools for treating a negative mind. In some people's cases, a lifestyle change is all they may need to recover from it. The following changes can help a person feel better physically, helping reduce the frequency of negative thoughts.

- **Exercise:** Researchers have found that regularly exercising can be an excellent repellent for negative thoughts.

Physical exercise boosts the 'feel-good' brain chemicals in the brain, such as serotonin and endorphins. These chemicals also trigger the growth of new brain cells and connections similar to what antidepressants do. The best part about exercise is that you don't need to do it intensely to benefit. Even a simple 30-minute walk can make a huge difference in a person's brain activity. For the best results, people should aim to do 30 – 60 minutes of aerobic activity every day or on most days.

- **Social Support:** As I mentioned earlier, having a strong social network reduces isolation, which is a huge risk factor in negative thinking. Make an effort to keep in regular contact with family and friends (ideally daily) and consider joining a support group or class. You can also opt to do some volunteering to get the social support you need while helping others.
- **Nutrition:** Healthy eating is important for everyone's mental and physical health. Eating well-balanced and small meals throughout the

day will help you minimize mood swings and keep energy levels up. Although you may crave sugary foods due to the quick boost they provide, complex carbohydrates are much more nutritious. They can provide you with an energy boost without a crash at the end.
- **Sleep:** A person's sleep cycle has strong effects on mood. When a person does not get enough sleep, their negative thinking styles may get worse. Sleep deprivation causes other negative symptoms like sadness, fatigue, moodiness, and irritability. Not many people can function well with less than seven hours of sleep per night. A healthy adult should be aiming for 7 – 9 hours of sleep every night.
- **Stress reduction:** When a person is suffering from too much stress, it exacerbates their depression and puts them at a higher risk of developing more serious depressive disorders.

Try to make changes in your life that can help you reduce or manage stress. Identify which aspects of your life creates the most stress, such as unhealthy relationships or work overload, and find ways to minimize their impact and the stress it brings.

Chapter 6: How Emotional Intelligence Will Help You

Throughout this chapter, we will look at what emotional intelligence is and how you can improve your emotional intelligence. This chapter will help you learn how improving your emotional intelligence will help you better understand others and understand yourself, avoiding worrying about what others may be feeling/thinking about you.

What Is Emotional Intelligence?

I will begin by describing what emotional intelligence is and how it affects you in your day to day life. We define emotional intelligence as a person's ability to recognize, understand, and control their emotions. Also, it includes a person's ability to recognize, understand, and influence other people's emotions. In the simplest terms, EI is the ability to be aware that emotions drive human behaviors and have the power to impact other people. By learning how to manage your emotions, you will be able to impact yourself and others positively.

A person's emotional intelligence comprises five distinct factors:

- a person's self-awareness
- a person's self-regulation
- a person's motivation

- a person's empathy
- a person's social skills

We will look at each of these factors individually to better understand the significance of emotional intelligence.

Self-Awareness

The first proponent of emotional intelligence is self-awareness. Simply put, self-awareness is being aware of the 'self.' We began to study self-awareness as a psychological study back in 1972. Psychologists concluded that when we focus our attention on our inner selves, we can evaluate and compare our current behavior to the standards and values we hold for ourselves. We become self-conscious and become objective evaluators of our actions. Becoming an objective evaluator is beneficial as it helps us see our behavior from an outside perspective and adjust it according to our values and standards.

Self-awareness allows people to understand their strengths and weaknesses. This understanding gives them a better grasp on how to react properly to other people in certain situations. When a person reflects on their emotions, they begin to gain self-awareness.

To grow emotional intelligence, a person will need to think about their feelings and react to negative situations or conflict situations. When a person becomes more aware of which emotions they are experiencing, they can begin to appropriately manage and control these emotions, leading to a higher self-awareness level.

As we saw above, Psychologists concluded that self-awareness is the foundation of self-control. Therefore, self-awareness is part of the foundation of Emotional Intelligence as well.

Self-awareness goes way beyond just gaining knowledge about ourselves. It also includes paying attention to our inner state and wellbeing with an open mind and heart. Our mind is exceptional at storing information and memories about how we react to certain situations to form a blueprint of our emotional life. Such information ends up training our mind to react the same way when we encounter similar situations in the future. Being self-aware allows us to be aware of the mind's conditioning and training, which can be the stepping stone to freeing the mind.

So, does self-awareness matter? According to psychologists, self-awareness is the cornerstone to achieving emotional intelligence. The ability to monitor and control our thoughts and feelings from minute to minute is important to understanding ourselves more, being comfortable with who we are, and proactively organizing our thoughts, behaviors, and emotions. Additionally, self-aware people act consciously rather than passively, and usually have good mental well-being and a positive view of life. They also tend to have larger and deeper life experience and are likely to be more compassionate. A scientific study in 2016 studied the parts of self-awareness and the benefits. They found that mindfulness, insight, and self-reflection are all aspects of self-awareness and lead to benefits like; becoming a more accepting person and harboring less emotional burdens such as overthinking and experiencing anxiety.

Self-Regulation

When a person can self-regulate, they have a higher level of Emotional Intelligence because they can properly regulate their emotions and keep themselves in check when needed.

Whether you are feeling angry or just in a conflict with another person, it is important to know how to conduct yourself maturely and effectively. Understanding this will allow you to get the most out of the interaction without causing undue damage to your mental health or relationships. Increasing your emotional intelligence level requires you to work on your ability to regulate your emotions and control them when need-be.

Suppose you are a person who tends to act on your feelings of anger with aggression, verbal outbursts, or even physical violence. In that case, these techniques will prove quite useful in your journey of finding higher emotional intelligence and freedom from overthinking after the fact. The skill of self-regulation will save your relationships and prevent you from acting out in ways that will harm your life. Sometimes we tend to act out in aggression or anger and then become self-conscious afterward, wondering if we were "too much" or "too harsh." If you are a person who tends to overthink, you could drive yourself mad, thinking back on your interaction after you act out in anger. By developing better self-regulation, you can prevent this and avoid suffering from overthinking-induced anxiety later on.

Motivation

The relationship that motivation has to emotional intelligence is threefold. The first is that having a high level of emotional intelligence will bring you more motivation. Thus, increasing your emotional intelligence will bring you motivation. The second is that people who have more motivation and a higher level of emotional intelligence are more optimistic. The third is that people who are more optimistic and have a higher level of emotional intelligence tend to be more resilient to negativity.

People who are prone to overthinking tend to lack the motivation to achieve their goals. This lack of motivation is because they spend most of their time analyzing every little thing that they use up all their energy and brainpower. That leaves them with lackluster motivation and causes them to feel bad about themselves. For this reason, working on increasing your motivation will help you to increase your emotional intelligence and break free from overthinking. We will look at this in more detail in the next chapter of this book, so stay tuned!

Empathy

People who are successful in connecting emotionally with others usually exhibit strong traits of empathy and compassion. Empathy is quite necessary for problem-solving and conflict resolution, as it enables you to solve with compassion instead of anger. There are three types of empathy, which we will look at below.

· Affective Empathy
Affective empathy is the ability to share someone else's feelings. It is also the ability to understand the feelings of another. It also involves responding according to this shared emotion.

· Somatic Empathy
The next type of empathy is called somatic empathy. This type of empathy involves a real, physical reaction to someone else's feelings. For example, if you see that your friend is embarrassed, and your face starts to turn red out of second-hand embarrassment.

· Cognitive Empathy
The third and final type of empathy is cognitive empathy. This type of empathy is when you can understand another person's feelings to understand

their mental state when feeling that emotion and imagine what they may be thinking or what their thought process may be.

The most common form of empathy, affective empathy (hereafter, empathy), is the ability that a person has to share someone else's feelings. It is also the ability to understand the feelings of another. The difference between empathy and sympathy is that sympathy only involves feeling sorry for someone else's feelings. In contrast, empathy involves putting yourself in their shoes to feel what they must be feeling.

Having a high level of emotional intelligence involves being in touch with yourself and the other person (or people) that you are communicating with. To do this, you will need to use empathy. Empathy will help you take responsibility for yourself, your actions, and your reactions and demonstrate a genuine interest in the other person/people. Empathy will help you develop a deeper understanding of people's motivations and what they do not say, informing their actions and reactions. By understanding this, you can connect with people and understand them while helping them understand you.

Empathy is important because of the way that it gets a person to understand the needs of others. This understanding is beneficial in problem-solving, as well as everyday interactions. Empathetic people express genuine interest in helping others and come from a place of understanding. In interactions with an empathetic person, each person can fully understand and connect with the other person's needs and help them get what they need. Empathy improves your interactions with others by helping you solve the situation to everyone's satisfaction. You will resolve things because you will be using empathy to understand the other person throughout your interaction. This method will result in empathy being carried on into other parts of your life, which will benefit your relationships and your overall daily life.

All of our discussion of empathy leads us to compassion. Compassion is a "higher-level emotion," meaning that it requires a person to be wise and more emotionally mature to experience it. Compassion is a form of empathy, meaning that it is a very similar emotion. The difference is that compassion is empathy without being overtaken or overwhelmed by another person's feelings. This difference means that it is the feeling of empathy but a more refined form. The benefit is that compassion is an emotion that a person can always find within them. They can find this in every interaction and with every person. In contrast, empathy can become overwhelming and exhausting if you feel it in every interaction you have.

Social Skills

A person who has a high level of emotional intelligence possesses the social skills needed to showcase their respect and care for others. For this reason, those who have higher EI tend to get along better with people in general.

Having a high level of EI will help your relationships in numerous ways. In addition to the conflict resolution skills that it will bring you, it will also lead to a better ability to connect with other people. Having a better social life as an optimistic person is probably obvious at this point. People typically want to be around other positive people and often avoid those who are negative.

Naturally, most people want to spend their time with optimistic people as they tend to be more cheerful and upbeat. They make better supporters and help encourage their friends to be better versions of themselves. Negative people tend to have a negative outlook on their own life, extending over to having a negative outlook on other people's lives. Generally, most people don't want to spend time with those who bring them down and feel negative about their lives. Even negative people prefer to spend time with positive people. Having more positive thinking allows you to attract other positive thinkers to generate motivation and inspiration to achieve bigger and better things in life.

By working on your social skills, this will allow you to understand others and your interactions with them better, reducing your risk of falling into the trap of overthinking.

How Emotional Intelligence Benefits You

As I mentioned at the beginning of this chapter, one of the most important skills to learn is emotional intelligence. Emotional Intelligence benefits you for several reasons; most of these reasons stem from the ability to read and understand others' behavior, reducing the risk of overthinking.

- It will help you to read people.

It is important to understand how to read people at the most basic human connection level and understand their motivations. Reading people will help you in knowing how to approach people and connect to them. We will look at an example of this to help you better understand the importance of emotional intelligence. If you are looking to get directions from a stranger on the street, you will need to read all of the people around you to determine who will be the most approachable person to ask.

To do this, you will need to take stock of several things about each person you see, including their body language and their overall energy, to find someone that appears more friendly so you can ask them for directions. You would want to be able to read the body language of someone who looks unhappy or angry, as that is a person you may not want to approach in the middle of the street.

- It will help you to read and understand social encounters.

By increasing your emotional intelligence level and learning to read people better, you can advance your life in many ways. For instance, if you seek promotion from your boss, you may be able to read their body language, verbal and non-verbal messages, and their overall mood to determine if it's the right time to ask for a promotion or a raise.

You can determine what more your boss wants to see from you to improve your performance or gain a promotion at a lower level.

- It will help you with dating and relationships. The above is also true for other types of relationships, such as a romantic relationship. If you are romantically interested in someone, properly analyzing them will allow you to understand what your relationship with them is like in their eyes. By assessing your relationship's level and strength, you may be better able to ask them out on a date or to initiate more conversations with them.

- It will help you to communicate better. Increasing your emotional intelligence level will give you the knowledge you will need to tailor your communication style to fit the exchange type. Tailoring allows you to grow closer with people and to build more rapport.

For instance, you wouldn't talk to your significant other in the way that you would talk to your boss. Learning to tailor your communication and entire demeanor to match the situation and the relationship is crucial for finding the right response to someone. If you notice that your boss looks unhappy, stressed, and angry that day by assessing his facial expression and posture, you may not want to approach him with a 3-week vacation request that day. Most people can read the situation and choose another day where their boss is in a better mood to ask for a favor. This book will teach you the tools and skills needed to assess anyone you want so you can find the right moments to ask for what you need and to further your desired relationships.

- It will help you to read people's personalities. Emotional intelligence will help you in your social interactions and relationships by giving you the ability to understand the different personality types that humans may exhibit. By gaining the ability to read and understand different personality types, you will be able to better connect with people in your life.

You have surely heard and used the term *personality* before, but we will begin by ensuring our definitions of the word *personality* are the same before we move on. The definition of the term personality and what it means varies greatly depending on who you ask. Still, in general, personality is a way of describing one's potential behaviors and actions in any given situation. Determining someone's personality and even your own can give you insight into how and why you or another person may act. In a way, it is a description of your character as it examines and explains your thoughts, behaviors, and feelings.

Understanding personality types is one of the most important benefits of increasing your level of emotional intelligence. This understanding allows you to account for natural differences in the way people act or display behavior simply because of what type of person they are.

How To Increase Your Emotional Intelligence

Throughout the remainder of this chapter, we will look at some strategies that will help you increase your level of emotional intelligence, leading to freedom from overthinking. If you struggle with this, take extra time to read through this chapter and practice the techniques outlined here the next time you feel like you may spiral into the anxiety of overthinking.

- What Not To Do

The first step in knowing how to do something is knowing how *not* to do it. Therefore, to begin, we will look at how not to conduct yourself when you feel the anger building.

a. Blame the Other Person
Often, blaming is what people do when they are afraid of looking bad or being blamed for something. This act does lead to a circular blaming game where everyone is blaming somebody, and the entire situation becomes a game of passing the blame like a hot potato. It may seem like being the one person who

doesn't take part in this game will make you look guilty, but it doesn't work this way. You will be open and vulnerable by opting out of the game and expressing yourself using NVC's four steps without inserting yourself into a losing game.

a. Threaten

Threatening is another way that you do not want to conduct yourself. By threatening, people will often then write off the conversation because they feel like you are pushing them into a corner. You don't want to make someone feel like this if you hope to get some sort of resolution from the interaction.

a. Guilt-Tripping

Guilt-tripping is another way that people often try to get a specific outcome from an interaction. This act leaves the other person feeling terrible about themselves and will leave you feeling negative about yourself. Guilt-tripping is not an effective way to resolve a situation, leading to resentment and stored anger.

a. Yelling

Yelling may feel like the way to get your point across, but when people are getting yelled at, they often shut down and stop listening, which then has the opposite effect than you aimed for. Raising your voice is inevitable sometimes, but what matters is the intent behind it. If you are doing it to force the person to see your perspective or yelling over them to listen to you, this will not help resolve any sort of conflict. People will also feel like you are attacking them when they are being yelled at, causing them to shut down, and the chance of resolution becomes zero.

a. Refuse to Take Responsibility
Finally, when people refuse to take responsibility for their anger and the way they acted out in anger, they often resort to blaming others for their decisions or shortcomings, failing to speak up when necessary, and complaining about situations, events, and decisions of others.

- What To Do

Assume Responsibility
The first thing that you want to do when conducting yourself maturely and effectively is assuming responsibility. Assuming responsibility means taking control of the part you play in a situation. It also means accepting the fact that you made the decisions you made, including any consequences that came with it.

Assuming responsibility is often hard to do, especially when assuming responsibility may mean looking bad in front of your boss or accepting that you made the decision, which caused something negative to happen. However, assuming responsibility brings you the respect of the people around you and allows you to live truthfully and genuinely. By doing this, you are transparent with others, which is a very respectable quality—having this quality will lead others to trust you and to thank you for your honesty. They will remember this characteristic that you possess, which will help you in many areas of your life. This benefit also goes for yourself. When something happens that may not be your desired outcome, accepting the fact that you made the decision that led to it but moving on from it and not blaming yourself or guilt-tripping yourself will help you learn from your mistakes. This process is taking responsibility for your decisions.

If you are unsure how to tell whether you are taking responsibility for your actions or how to do so in the future, one of the best ways to do this is to recognize that you have choices. Many times, our reasoning for things is that "I had no choice." We all know that this could not be farther from the truth. This narrative is one that we use when we do not want to take responsibility for our actions or decisions, as it makes us feel better to think that we had no other option. The reality is that we always have a choice, and we always have options. The sooner you recognize this, the better off you will be in life, and the sooner you will be assuming responsibility. By understanding that you always have a choice and that this choice is yours to make, you live authentically.

1. Learn from Your Mistakes
Once you assume responsibility, you can then learn from your mistakes. Only then can you begin to learn from them. If you do not accept responsibility for your decisions or choices, you will not ever feel like you have made a mistake.

Assuming responsibility comes with standing by the decisions you made, which, in hindsight, may not have been the ones that you would make again. This difference is what sets those who assume responsibility apart from those who do not. Stand by your decision even when it does not lead to the ideal outcome and choose to learn from mistakes.

Without taking responsibility, you will never learn from your mistakes; you need to recognize that you made a mistake to learn from it.

You may be wondering what learning from your mistakes looks like in practice. I will walk you through a step-by-step process that will help you to understand this better below.

Step 1: Recognize the Existence of a Mistake
As I mentioned, the first step in learning from your mistakes recognizes that you made one. Once you do this, you are ready to let it teach you a lesson and make you a better person. This steps may be the most difficult one, but it is the most important.

Step 2: Recognize the Decision or Choice that Leads to it.
Once you have recognized a mistake, you can work backward to determine what choice or decision led to the mistake. Many times, multiple decisions lead up to an event or occurrence, so pinpointing, which resulted in the mistake, will help you learn from it.

Step 3: Recognize the Thought Process that Leads to it.

Once you have pinpointed the decision that leads to a mistake, think back on your thought process when making that choice. Once you do this, you can see the point where you may have made an error in judgment or now see the decision more clearly. Going back to the thought process, you can intervene at the exact spot where you would change the next time when faced with a similar decision. Once you determine the point where you would make a different choice along the decision-making process, you can then see how every thought or choice after that would be different. This act can lead you to see what final decision this would have resulted in.

Step 4: Think About your Ideal Result
Thinking about what you hoped for in terms of an ideal result can help you in that you will work backward and determine what sequence of decisions or thought processes would have led to this ideal result. It is important to recognize that sometimes the results are out of your hands and that you can only do so much to try to make a certain result happen. By recognizing this, you can prepare as best you can for this result, but you won't beat yourself up if factors that are genuinely out of your control determine the result. For example, if you have an audition coming up and choose a song to perform. You can do everything you can to decide which song you will choose and prepare for the audition, but the choice is out of your hands at the end of the day. Suppose the audition does not go well, and this is due to your song choice. In that case, you can use the steps above to determine where you went wrong in your decision-

making process and what you would change the next time. Still, you must also recognize that even if you made these changes next time, the final result is due to others' decision-making.

Step 5: Plan for Next Time
When you are looking ahead to the next time you will make a similar decision, think about your goals in terms of the situation. This step will help you to make the best choices you can along the way.

Step 6: Repeat
If the situation (or a similar one) occurs again and you still do not get a result that you want, begin again learning from your mistakes. There is no limit to the number of times you can learn from your mistakes, and the more you do so, the better off you will be in your life.

Every person has made many mistakes, but what is important is not the number of mistakes you have made. What is important is how much you take away from these situations to help you in later scenarios and situations. If you are constantly making mistakes and learning from them, you will be much better off and closer to achieving your goals than a person who makes few mistakes but never takes responsibility for the ones they do make. Remember this as you go through your life, as it is important not only with anger management but also in every life area.

- Build more empathy by making a point to understand the 'why' behind somebody's emotions or feelings.

- Try to step into the other person's shoes: Imagine how it would feel to be them in this situation or any given situation.

- Chose to learn from criticism:
Nobody likes criticism, but it is an inevitable part of life. Decide to learn from criticism rather than jumping into defense mode; this way, you can improve your emotional intelligence.

- Practice Honest Self-Expression:
Honest self-expression is what comes as a result of practicing effective communication.

We define honest self-expression as expressing oneself authentically in a way that is likely to inspire compassion in others. Expressing your true feelings and ensuring that your feelings are the deepest ones you could find is quite intimidating and can make you feel extremely vulnerable. Connecting this deep feeling to a need or a value you hold requires yet another level of vulnerability. Sharing your needs and values is likely not something that you often do.

By sharing these things at one time is sure to make you feel very vulnerable. These two things are both ways of expressing yourself authentically. Therefore, you are practicing honest self-expression. Deciding to be vulnerable, even though it is hard and uncomfortable, inspires compassion in others for a few reasons.

The first reason is that they can see you deciding to be vulnerable and open to your feelings. Everyone can relate to how difficult this is, which makes them feel empathy or compassion for you in this situation. Second, because you are expressing a need and know that this is a difficult thing to do, they will also feel empathy or compassion for this need, as being vulnerable shows them that this is important to you.

If you are a victim of overthinking, emotional intelligence is an area you need to understand better why you feel your emotions. If you are overthinking what others are thinking about you, emotional intelligence can help you better read. Individuals who have higher emotional intelligence tend to live a happier life outside of the workplace due to lower risk of disorders like depression and anxiety.

Below I have included a few additional ways that a person can work to improve their emotional intelligence:

- Reflect on your emotions: When a person reflects on their emotions, they begin to gain self-awareness. To grow emotional intelligence, start by thinking about your feelings and think about how you tend to react to negative situations. When you become more aware of which emotions you are dealing with, you can begin to manage and control them appropriately.

- Ask for another perspective: Everyone's perception of reality is different. Start by asking others for their opinions and understanding what you are like during emotionally charged situations.

- Observe: Once you have started being more self-aware, try to understand your behavior better. Begin to observe your emotions and pay attention to them.

- Pause for a moment: Stop to think about what emotions you feel before you act. It may be difficult to do this in emotionally heated situations, but it will become a habit with practice.

- Practice: Improving emotional intelligence does not happen overnight; however, it is proven to improve with some practice.

Chapter 7: How Self-Discipline Will Help You

Remember when we discussed motivation in the previous chapter? Here is where we will revisit it and look at how you can increase your motivation through self-discipline. People who are prone to overthinking lack the motivation to achieve their goals. This lack of motivation is because they spend most of their time analyzing every little thing that they use up all their energy and brainpower. That leaves them with lackluster motivation and causes them to feel bad about themselves.

To overcome overthinking, increasing your self-discipline to create motivation can help you to begin spending your time reaching your goals rather than thinking about everything that could go wrong with them. This chapter will explore methods of improving self-discipline, creating motivation, and overcoming procrastination.

Improving Self-Discipline Is A Necessity

Understanding the psychology behind self-discipline is extremely crucial as it will help you learn what the driving factors are behind it. One of the main factors that drive self-discipline is willpower. A common belief in people is that they think they can change their lives for the better if they simply could have more willpower. If people had more willpower, everyone would save responsibly for retirement, exercise regularly, stop procrastinating, stop overthinking, avoid alcohol and drugs, and achieve all kinds of noble goals. One survey that studied all Americans and their annual stress found that most participants reported that lacking willpower is the number one reason for not following the changes they want for themselves.

What Is The Driving Factor Behind Self-Discipline?

As you just learned, willpower is the main driving factor behind self-discipline. Working on your willpower is the one-way ticket for you to achieve self-discipline. In the survey that we just mentioned, results showed that the biggest obstacle to people achieving change was the lack of willpower. Even though many people often blame the scarcity of their willpower for their unhealthy choices, they are still grasping on to the hope of achieving it one day. Most people in this study also reported that they think willpower can be taught and learned. They are correct.

Some research has recently discovered many examples of how people can strengthen willpower with training and practice. On the contrary, some survey participants expressed that they think they would have more willpower if they had more free time to spare. However, the willpower concept isn't something that increases automatically if a person has more time in their day. That leads me to the next question: How can people resist when they are facing temptation? Over the last several years, researchers made many discoveries about how willpower works by scientists worldwide. We will dive a little deeper into what our current understanding of willpower is.

Weak willpower isn't the only reason for a person to fail at achieving their goals. Psychologists in the field of willpower have built three crucial components when it comes to achieving goals. They said that you first need to set a clear goal and then establish the motivation for change. They said the second component was to monitor your behavior in regards to that goal. Willpower itself is the third and final component. If your goal is similar to the following; stop smoking, get fit, study more, or stop wasting time on the internet, willpower is an important concept to understand if you are looking to achieve any of those goals.

The bottom line of willpower is achieving long-term goals by resisting temporary temptations and urges. Here are several reasons why this is beneficial. Over a regular school year, psychologists performed a study that examined the self-control in a class of eighth-grade students. The researchers in this study did an initial assessment of the students' self-discipline by getting them, their parents, and teachers to fill out a questionnaire. They took it one step further and gave these students the task of deciding whether they want to receive $1 right away or $2 if they waited a week.

At the end of the study, the results pointed out that the students who had better test scores, better school attendance, better grades, and had a higher chance of being admitted to competitive high school programs all ranked high on the self-discipline assessment. These researchers found that self-discipline played a bigger role than IQ when it came to predicting academic success. Other studies have found similar evidence. In a different study, researchers asked a group of undergraduate university students to fill out self-discipline questionnaires that assessed their self-control. These researchers developed a scale that helped score the students on to the strength of their willpower. They found that the students with higher self-esteem, better relationship skills, higher GPA, and less alcohol or drug abuse had the highest self-control scores from the questionnaire.

Another study found that the benefits of willpower tend to be relevant well past university years. Researchers conducted this self-control study on 1000 people who they tracked since birth to the age of 32. This study was a long-term study in New Zealand, where they wanted to learn more about the effects of self-control well into adulthood. They found that the people who had high self-control during their childhood grew up into adults with better mental and physical health. They also had fewer substance abuse problems, criminal convictions, better financial security, and better money-saving habits. These patterns were proven even after the researchers had adjusted external influences such as socioeconomic factors, general intelligence, and these people's home lives. These findings prove why willpower is extremely important in almost all areas of a person's life.

Now that you have learned the importance of willpower and its role in multiple stages of a person's life let's define it a little further. There are many other names used for willpower that we can use interchangeably. These names include; drive, determination, self-control, resolve, and self-discipline.

Some psychologists will characterize willpower in even more specific ways. Some define willpower to be:

- The capacity to overcome unwanted impulses, feelings, or thoughts.
- The ability to resist temporary urges, temptation and delay instant gratification to achieve goals that are more long-term
- The effortful and conscious regulation of oneself.
- The ability to engage a "cool" cognitive system of behavior rather than a "hot" emotional system
- A limited resource that can be depleted

You can use willpower to achieve your goals, but you can also stop yourself from overthinking. However, this will draw from your willpower resources, and you may fall back into old back habits if you are tired from exerting your willpower. Instead, let's take a look at how you can create motivation and self-discipline so you can avoid using up your willpower resources and stop your overthinking in other ways instead.

How To Improve Your Self-Discipline (10-Step Guide)

You can do things to learn self-discipline and tap into your will power source to live a happier life. Below are ten steps that you should follow to master your self-discipline over ten days.

Step 1: Figure out your weaknesses.

Everyone has their own set of weaknesses. They could range from a certain type of food like chocolate, or it can be social media like Instagram, or even the latest addictive video game. Regardless of what it is, it has a similar effect on everyone.

The first step to mastering your self-discipline is acknowledging your shortcomings, no matter what they might be. People often try to pretend that their weaknesses don't exist to portray themselves as a strong person. This act that people put on is extremely ineffective when it comes to self-discipline. The purpose of acknowledging your weaknesses is not to make yourself feel bad. Instead, it helps you recognize what they are and will help you plan to overcome them. Acknowledge your flaws. It is impossible to overcome them until you do this.

Step 2: Eliminate your temptations.

Once you have acknowledged your weaknesses, you can now move on to step two, remove your temptations. Like we mentioned in step one, everyone has their own set of weaknesses, and it can range from small things like an unhealthy snack to something that hinders your productivity, like playing a video game for hours on end. By understanding your weaknesses, you can make accommodations for yourself to help remove some of those temptations.

For example, if somebody is looking to lose weight and get fit at the gym, but they know that their weakness is that they always eat chocolate after dinner every night. In this case, their temptation removal would be not to buy any more chocolate to keep around in their home. By not having chocolate in the home, they would be unable to fall into the temptation of eating it, which will hinder their progress of getting fit. However, this does not mean that they will never be able to eat chocolate again. It only means that they can indulge in their favorite snacks when they have achieved a certain portion of their goal. Rewarding oneself is important to self-discipline, as well.

Step 3: Define your goals and create an action plan.

To continue strengthening your self-discipline, a person must have a clear vision of what goals they are trying to accomplish. They must also have an understanding of what success means to them. If a person doesn't know where they're planning to go or what accomplishing their goals even and Tails, it is easy for them to lose their way or get sidetracked.

Make sure the goals that you are setting have a clear and concise purpose. For example, don't use goals like "I want to be successful in the next five years." This goal is too broad for it to have a strong meaning. Instead, you should make a quantifiable goal like, "I am planning on graduating from college in two years." Then, when you have a quantifiable goal, you can make a plan that makes sense for yourself.

For example, you can plan to study hard and get an A on each test for the remainder of the year to reach the goal- achieving a high GPA by the end. They can break down these goals even further and figure out where in their schedule they can add study hours or how they can get even closer to accomplishing that goal.

Step 4: Start to build upon your self-discipline.

Self-discipline is not something that people are born with; it is instead a learned behavior. Self-discipline is just like any other skill that people may be looking to grow; it requires repetition and daily practice. Like going to the gym, the more you work out your muscles, the bigger and stronger they will become. Changes do not happen overnight; instead, to strengthen your muscles and grow them, it will take at least several weeks for a person to see their progress. The effort and focus that training self-discipline requires can be extremely tiring.

The more time you spend practicing self-discipline, the more difficult it can become to keep utilizing your willpower. Sometimes, when a person faces a big temptation or decision, they may feel that overcoming that large temptation makes it harder for them to overcome other tasks requiring self-discipline. The only way to move past this is to have a good mindset. By having a good mindset, it creates a buffer for how quickly your willpower becomes drained. Also, like the muscle example we used, by exerting your willpower more often, you will have a higher tolerance and therefore be able to exert it more than if you were just starting.

Step 5: Build new habits and keep everything simple.

To strengthen self-discipline, you need to instill a new habit, which can feel very intimidating at first, especially if you focus on the entire goal all at once. To avoid this daunting feeling:
1. Keep it very simple.
2. Break your bigger goal into smaller doable ones.
3. Instead of trying to accomplish one huge goal immediately or to change all of your habits all at once, focus on doing just one thing consistently and exercise your self-discipline with that one small thing.

For example, if you are looking to get into better shape, start exercising for 10 to 15 minutes per day. Instead of trying to go to the gym for 2 hours every day, which can be very daunting, start with a smaller goal in mind first. By taking baby steps, you can get your mind used to that habit and slowly increase the amount of time you spend at the gym. Eventually, once you feel like that goal has become a habit, you can then begin to focus on other small goals and keep building up words from there.

Step 6: Adopt healthy eating habits.

In the earlier chapters, we learned that glucose levels play a big role in a person's brainpower, which controls a person's willpower. The sensation of being hungry can cause people to feel angry, annoyed, and irritated. This feeling is real, and everyone has felt it before and often has a huge impact on a person's willpower. Research has found evidence that having low blood sugar weakens a person's ability to make good decisions.

When a person is hungry, their ability to concentrate suffers greatly, and their brains don't function optimally. Therefore, a person's self-control is likely to be weakened when their body is in this state. To prevent this, make sure to constantly eat small meals to prevent yourself from feeling that annoying hungry feeling causes people to have a lapse in judgment. Since exercising willpower takes up a lot of energy from a person's brain, make sure to keep fuelling it with enough glucose so that the brain can keep functioning at an optimal level.

Step 7: Get rid of any negative preconceptions you have with willpower.

In the earlier chapters, we learned that a person's perspective or beliefs could buffer how long it takes to have their willpower drained completely. Although most researchers believe that there is a limit to how much we can tap into our willpower, they also found that the people who believe that there wasn't a limit had a bigger will power stockpile. If a person believes that they have limited willpower, they probably will not surpass those limits. However, if a person does not place a strict limit on themselves, they are less likely to use up their willpower stockpile before meeting their goals.

A person's internal perception about their willpower and self-control plays a huge role in determining how much willpower they have. If a person can remove these obstacles by believing that they have a large stockpile of willpower and believing in themselves, they are less likely to drain out their willpower than someone who believes that they don't have much of it. So try changing your perception of how you see your willpower. Try to think of it as a source that can run out, but you have a larger amount of it because of your beliefs. This mindset is a much better mindset than thinking that willpower will run out, so you should be stingy with it.

Step 8: Create a backup plan.

Many psychologists use a famous technique that helps with boosting willpower called "implementation intention." This technique is where you give yourself a plan when you are facing a potentially difficult situation.

We will revisit the example that we used earlier. Suppose a person is trying to reduce the amount of alcohol they drink, and they receive an invitation to a party where they will face alcohol. This situation could cause a person to feel extreme anxiety if they attend this part without a plan. In this case, before they go to the party, they will plan to ask for a plain soda with lime instead of asking for a beer like they normally would.

By making a plan before going into a situation where you know you will face big temptations, you will have an action plan. When you have an action plan, you can automatically execute this plan when you find yourself in that situation, rather than having to come up with an excuse on the spot and risking failure. For example, in the scenario, we looked at above. If the person went to the party without a plan, they would face people handing them alcoholic drinks or asking them if they wanted a beer. Instead of entering the party and immediately getting a soda with lime, they can avoid the questions and temptations that would come with entering without a plan.

When a person goes into those situations with a plan, it helps give them the mindset and self-control necessary to overcome obstacles. They will save energy by not making sudden decisions or making sudden plans based on their emotional state. This preparation will make them less likely to cave into temptations and more likely exercise their self-discipline.

Step 9: Don't forget to reward yourself.

Like anything else in life, it is necessary to give yourself a break and reward yourself. Give yourself something to look forward to by planning an appropriate reward when you accomplish your goals. This reward plan is not much different from when you were a little kid, and you got a treat from your parents for showing good behavior. When a person has something to look forward to, it gives them the extra motivation to succeed.

Anticipation is a powerful thing. It gives people something to focus on so that they are not only thinking of all the things they need to change.

When you have achieved one of your goals, you can find yourself a new goal and a new reward to keep motivating yourself to move forward. However, the reward should not be something unhealthy.

For example, in the previous example of the person trying to lower their alcohol intake, their reward for reducing their alcohol intake should not be something like allowing themselves to binge drink the following Friday. Their reward should be something healthy that won't make them lose progress on all the work that they've done. For example, this reward could be dinner at a nice restaurant or a new video game. Now, for a person trying to get active and lose weight, a new video game would not be an ideal reward. Instead, their reward should be something like attending a sports match or spending time in a social setting.

Step 10: Forgive your failures and keep moving forward.

Even if a person has all the best intentions and the most well-made plans, sometimes they will fall short when practicing self-discipline. Avoiding failure altogether is impossible, and we should not build a mindset around that. Everyone will have their ups and downs, their successes, and their failures.

The key to overcoming the failures that you will face is simply to keep moving forward. If you stumble on your self-discipline journey, instead of giving up altogether, acknowledge what caused it, learn from it, and then move on. Don't let yourself get caught up in frustration, anger, or guilt because these emotions are the ones that will de-motivate you and get in the way of your future progress. Learn from the mistakes you have made and be comfortable with forgiving yourself. Once you have done that, you can get your head back in the game and start where you left off.

Changing Your Mindset Regarding Motivation

People often have the wrong mindset where they think that they need to feel fully motivated before they start working on a task/job. This mindset is unrealistic. People's motivation often does not arrive until they have started that task and are beginning to see progress. When people see progress, they start to see the fruits of their labor, and they become even more motivated to keep working until they have completed their task. You might be wondering, "what about the motivation that is needed to start working altogether?" The answer to this is the following;
A person needs a good understanding of the 'why' and a strong vision before beginning. They should know what the benefits are going to be. You would be surprised at how many people waste a lot of time doing work they do not need to complete.

Moreover, people should be using prioritization to get the most urgent and important work out of the way first. By understanding the benefits of completing a task or job, you will fully understand its importance. In terms of smaller tasks/jobs, simply understanding the benefits of completing that task should be enough for motivation. For larger tasks and jobs, you must have a way to measure your progress to gain motivation and confidence from your work further.

How To Stop Overthinking To Overcome Procrastination

Procrastination is often something that those who overthink a lot suffer from. One of the biggest steps in overcoming your habit of overthinking is to beat your procrastination. You may think that you are only procrastinating because of your lack of motivation. However, we learned that motivation is something that happens after you take action rather than before. To overcome procrastination, you can't sit around waiting for motivation to hit. You have to begin your task to create motivation. To start doing a task without motivation, you need to utilize your willpower and self-discipline. Let's take a look at 11 steps that we can take to overcome procrastination and begin creating motivation for ourselves.

Step 1: Break down your goals into smaller goals

People put off doing the work they need to do because they subconsciously find that their work is too overwhelming. Start by just breaking down whatever that task is into littler parts and then focus on one at a time. If you find yourself still wanting to procrastinate after you've already broken it down, then break it down even more. You will eventually get to a point where the task you need to do is so easy that you would feel very badly about yourself if you didn't just do it.

For example, imagine that one of your goals is to manage your money better. It is tax season, and you need to complete your taxes to understand your financial situation. Imagine that you are feeling overwhelmed as you don't even know where to begin filing your taxes. You are also afraid that you may owe money to the government that you might not have. Here is how I would break down the large and broad task of 'filing taxes':

1. Research the best way to file taxes for beginners
2. Explore my options (either downloading software for DIY or going to a tax filing company)
3. Pick which option suits you best
4. Gather the documents that are suggested based on which option you chose in step #2
5. Follow the instructions given to you by the tax software or the tax professional

Suddenly that one large task of 'filing taxes' became much more manageable. Instead of thinking about filing taxes as one large unit, you are now starting with a simple google search of the best way to file taxes for beginners. From there, now you can make an educated decision on which method is easiest for you to proceed with. By taking things one step at a time, your mind becomes less overwhelmed.

Step 2: Improve your working environment.

Different types of environments produce different impacts on a person's productivity. Take a look at your workspace, does looking at it make you want to go back to bed? Or does it look inviting enough to make you want to jump right into work? If it's the former, you may want to consider changing up your workspace to make it more inviting. For instance, I used to have stronger feelings of procrastination when I let my desk get cluttered. It did not look inviting, and in fact, it added stress as now I needed to clear up my workspace before doing a task that I didn't even really want to do in the first place. By keeping your workspace clean, tidy, and inviting, you can skip the step of having to tidy up before getting your hands dirty with work.

Step 3: Create detailed plans with actual deadlines

When a person just has one singular deadline for a large task, it's an invitation to procrastinate. This procrastination happens because people get under the impression that they have time and continue to keep pushing things back until the deadline is looming over them. In step one, we discussed breaking down your task into smaller ones. In this step, we will make our deadlines for each small task. The purpose of this is, so you have a general idea when you have to finish each task. If you don't finish one step by the deadline you have set, you jeopardize every step that you planned after that. This pressure helps create some urgency and forces you to finish everything on time.

Step 4: Get rid of any procrastination temptations.

If you are a constant procrastination offender, it may be because you make it very easy for yourself to be distracted. Be self-aware – what are the things you typically find yourself doing when you're supposed to be doing something else? Is it browsing the internet? Scrolling your phone? Identify what exactly it is that is tempting you to procrastinate and try to prevent yourself from being tempted in the first place. If you are easily distracted by your phone, turn it off for an hour, put it in a drawer, and begin to work. Some people may extreme and go as far as disabling all their social media accounts to prevent themselves from endless browsing. It doesn't have to be extremely drastic but take preventative measures, so it's not too easy for you to procrastinate.

Step 5: Network with people who inspire you

Choosing who you spend your time with heavily influences your behaviors. If you are spending time with people who procrastinate and don't see anything wrong with it, you are likely to think that that is okay. Instead, try to surround yourself with people that are motivated and have achieved many goals before. You will soon be able to gain some of their motivation and spirit as well.

Step 6: Get yourself a partner.

When you have a large set of tasks that you need to get done, having a friend or an acquaintance that can complete them with you will make the process much easier for both of you! When choosing a person to partner up with, it should ideally be someone that also has their own large set of tasks/goals that they want to complete. The reason for this is that you can hold each other accountable for the tasks that you need to do. This method will help you to avoid procrastination.

The two of you will hold each other accountable for the tasks that you each must do, even if those tasks are different from each other. You do not need to have the same goals as your partner, but you can!

Suppose you and your partner are working on two completely different goals, but you both complete small tasks daily that bring you closer to your end goals. It does not matter what those daily tasks are as long as you complete them.

For example, many people with goals of getting more fit or losing weight will find themselves a workout buddy or a partner that will help hold them accountable for going to the gym or planning workout sessions together. That way, if one of you doesn't feel like exercising or going to the gym the other person can motivate them to do it anyway.

Step 7: Share your goals with others

This step serves a similar function as the step before but on a much larger scale.

This step involves telling the people in your life about the goals that you hope to accomplish. If you are the only one who knows about your goals, there is nobody to check in on you and make sure that you are making progress.

This step works better if you tell your loved ones specific details about the goals you want to accomplish. These details can be things like the following:

- Your deadlines.
- The plan you've made for yourself.
- The steps that you will take along the way.
- The other people who are working towards these goals with you.
- The results that you hope to achieve at the end.
- The benefits that achieving this goal will bring to your life.
- And so on.

The next time you see these people, they will likely ask you what your status is on your goals. They will likely ask you for updates on your progress, or they may see changes in you and congratulate you on them. All of these things will create motivation for you, which will keep you on track.

Also, people tend not to want to 'fail' in front of others, so if you know that there are people who are following along with your journey, you are more likely to make sure that you have made some progress by the time they ask you for an update.

Another version of this would be posting updates about your journey to social media. If you post updates about your progress or your goals for the future on social media, people can get behind you and motivate you to keep going. If you post regular updates (daily or weekly) people will begin following along and they will be the motivation you need to keep going.

Step 8: Find someone who has achieved the same goal.

If your goal is one that you think other people have accomplished before, try to find out who these people are. Seek them out and connect with them to ask them about their experience. You can learn about what obstacles and failures they faced along the way, and they'd be able to provide you with some tips that may have made their journey a little bit easier. Moreover, seeing living proof that your goals are achievable ones may help you take action even sooner.

Step 9: Reassess your goals often.

If you are someone that has been procrastinating for a long time now, it might be due to the misalignment of what you're currently doing and what you want. People often outgrow their goals when they begin to learn more about themselves. However, they don't always adjust their goals based on those changes. Try to take a weekend to yourself and regroup. Ask yourself, 'what exactly do I want to achieve? Are the things that I am doing now aligning with that? If not, what can I do to change it?' Adjusting your goals to something that lines up with who you are presently is crucial in creating motivation and value.

Step 10: Keep things simple

There is never a 'perfect time' to do a task that you need to do. You may be identifying all the reasons why the present moment is 'not the best time,' but that is the wrong mindset to have. Even if you only had 10 minutes, you can surely get SOMETHING done related to your goal. Abandon this thought of waiting for 'the perfect time' because there will never be one. After you break down your goals into smaller ones, start doing them whenever you have 10 minutes free. It's as simple as that.

Step 11: Just Do It

At the end of it all, everything comes down to simply just taking action. Just like how we learned motivation comes from starting something and not before, simply taking the first step to doing something will create the motivation you need to keep you going. A person can do all the planning and strategizing they need, but nothing will happen if they don't take the first step.

Chapter 8: The Role Your Subconscious Mind Plays

In this chapter, we will look at the role that your subconscious mind plays in overthinking. I will begin by defining the different kinds of consciousness, and then we will look at the subconscious mind in particular.

The Conscious Mind

The conscious mind includes everything that you are aware of. This awareness includes your thoughts, your short-term memories, and anything that is currently occupying your mind.

The Subconscious Mind

On the other hand, the subconscious mind is the part of your consciousness without your knowledge. This mind includes things like memories, which are in your mind, which you are not currently aware of, but can be brought into your conscious mind any time you wish to access them.

The Inner Critic

Everybody has an inner critic. Your inner critic is the voice in "the back of your mind" that questions you and tells you things throughout the day. This act happens without any thought, meaning that this goes on in your subconscious mind. The challenge here is to begin recognizing your inner critic voice, bring it into your conscious mind, and then challenge and change the beliefs that it has.

Some people battle with their inner critic more than others. Your inner critic is responsible for any negative thoughts that go on through your head and may also affect your self-esteem. Your inner critic is also very responsible for a lot of the overthinking that you do.

Individuals who have low self-esteem tend to have very active and inaccurate inner critics. Therapies such as Cognitive Behavioral Therapy (CBT) effectively help people learn to start questioning what their inner critic is saying to them, rather than listening to it and accepting it.

For instance, an individual finds themselves thinking that they are useless. This feeling comes up because their inner critic is telling them so. Instead of accepting this and believing it, the goal is to notice these thoughts and question the inner critic. You can do this by saying something like, "What evidence is there that supports the accusation that I am a loser?" or "What evidence is there that doesn't support the accusation that I am a loser?"

Through this technique, people often find that there isn't much (or any) evidence that supports the negative statement that their inner critic said about them. The ability to catch themselves thinking these thoughts that have no supporting evidence is a sign that you have learned to question your inner critic.

For the rest of this chapter, we will be focusing on catching the times where our inner critic begins to say negative things about ourselves and then find a way to contradict those statements. This strategy will help you better manage your overthinking tendencies.

The first you need to take to tame your inner critic is to be aware of it simply. By being aware of it, you will need to be curious. Most people in modern-day society passively move through their lives. Due to how fast-paced things have become nowadays if we don't give our thoughts and feelings the attention it needs, we tend to forget about them. Even though everybody feels numerous emotions daily, they don't acknowledge them every time. Instead, people have learned to react to everything and turn on auto-pilot simply. When we do this, we don't question or evaluate the downsides to their actions and decisions.

Rather than falling back into old habits of ignoring or rejecting your inner critic, we will practice acknowledging it instead. People often resist thinking about a certain thing, but they just think about it more and have a larger effect on their lives. Rather than resisting this step, acknowledge the words of your inner critic instead. Try shifting your mind and think of your inner critic's words as opinions and concerns for your well-being rather than insults. Try to believe that your inner critic has the best intentions for you and is trying to help you. Although it may be hindering right now, your inner critic comes from a place of concern and care.

In the following exercise, start having a conversation with your inner critic, and then ask them the following questions. Feel free to write your answers down; figuring out your inner critic's true intentions is important in changing their words.

1. What is my inner-critic trying to protect me from?
2. What does my inner-critic not want me to feel or experience?
3. Why is this important to my inner-critic?
4. Are the words my inner-critic is using critical or constructive?
5. Are the words being used designed to help me improve or to criticize me?
6. Are the words being used based on factual evidence? Or are they based on an opinion?
7. If I consider these words, wherein my life might I need to make some changes?
8. How else could I make changes in my life without all this resistance from my inner-critic?

Below is a list of responses that you can employ by saying them to your inner critic when you hear its negative voice in your head.

- Stop saying the same negative statements about me. I have supporting evidence that I am not any of those things you are describing me as. I will change you to begin to tell me more positive and encouraging messages instead of negative ones.

- You are lying. I have evidence that does not support the statements you are saying about me. I've taken an objective look at myself, and I am not the things you are saying.

- I belong. You are mimicking the voice of the bullies in my childhood, and your words are false. I have grown up to be a respectful and good person.

- I am not weak. I have faced and conquered so many of my fears, and I plan on facing more of them. Your words do not have any supporting evidence.

- I am not scared. I have faced my fear head-on and conquered it. I will continue to do this.

- Stop beating me up. Stop hurting my esteem just because I don't want to have more negative thoughts. I will replace your negative words with positive thoughts about myself and my goals.

Chapter 9: Practical Methods To Stop Overthinking

In this final chapter, we will explore other methods that can help end your overthinking. Up to this point, we have learned how to manage your overthinking by using CBT, meditation, self-discipline, and improving your physical health. We will now focus on some less conventional methods that scientists proved to help manage to overthink.

Gratitude Practice

Increasing gratitude helps individuals have the ability to feel more positive emotions that are associated with having greater happiness. Being thankful for the things one has in life will help people shift their mindset away from the constant need to want things. There are many ways that you can practice gratitude daily. Take a few minutes every morning or before going to bed to write down five good things that happened in your day. Keep in mind that it doesn't have to be a major event (like winning a prize from a lottery ticket), but it can be simple things like having a good meal, the nice weather, or just having a good chat with a friend. Be as consistent as you can with this journal, as only doing it now and then won't be effective compared to doing this multiple times a week.

You can also go on a 'gratitude walk.' Go for a walk in your local neighborhood and make an effort to absorb and appreciate your surroundings. Try to notice things that you normally don't pay attention to, like the buildings around you, the smell of the air, or the nature around you. Spend a few minutes during your walk to solely focus on your senses (sight, touch, taste, smell, and hearing). Try to look for new things during your walk in your everyday environment that you normally don't pay attention to. Write down some new appreciations you may have discovered through this walk and how it affected your mood.

Talk To Yourself

Remind yourself that people don't care that much about the things you say and do.

It is very easy to trigger negative thinking when you think about what other people think or say about you. You may think that they have strong feelings towards everything you do. You then will spend a lot of attention on analyzing your every decision and move. Getting stuck in a negative state of mind will drag you into a field of negativity and away from your real goals.

The truth is, people don't have that much time, energy, or attention to pay attention to everything you think and do. Like you, they have their minds and hands full of their day-to-day responsibilities like their pets, kids, jobs, and their fears and worries.

Realizing that people don't care all that much about your actions will set yourself free from others' constraints. This thought will allow you to start making decisions for yourself and yourself only.

Make an effort to find things to like, appreciate and love

Rather than fighting negative thoughts, tooth and nail, consciously try to reach for more positive thoughts. A powerful way is to speak out loud about the things you like and love. Simple phrases such as "I love the way my coffee tastes this morning" or "I like today's weather" can help bring more positive thoughts to your mind. When you actively reach for relief, you will have an easier time finding it.

Ask yourself the hard questions.

Start thinking about what you have to gain when you are constantly thinking negative thoughts. What is in it for you? What do you get from these negative thought patterns? What do you lose when you have negative thinking? What is the cost of all this negativity? When you begin to think about what negative thinking is doing for you, you may realize that it is detrimental to your mental health and overall well-being.

Practice affirmations

When you wake up in the morning, try to feel the gratitude you have for today. Write down affirmations such as "I love my family" or "I make a positive impact on people's lives" or "I am open to inspiring others and being inspired." If a negative thought pops up in your mind, try to think of a positive event or success that you've had as well. Positive thinking is a daily task and is not something that just happens.

Do not underestimate the power of positive thinking. Affirmations are a concrete way to include positivity in your day by giving you something specific to say or do. Remember your affirmations, and they will automatically fill you with positivity. Some more examples of affirmations are below;

- I am beautiful
- I am grateful for my dog
- I love my friends
- Life is sweet
- I am capable and strong

Conclusion

I would like to take this time to congratulate you on reaching the end of this book. Reading the entirety of it was not an easy task, as it required a lot of self-reflection and digging deep. Take some time to be proud of yourself for this feat.

This process is tiring, and many people give up halfway as they are not comfortable getting to know themselves. Getting to know yourself means you will learn fallbacks about who you are. However, you also learn about all the positive traits and features that make who you are today. The reality is that overthinking is something that will never entirely go away. You may overcome it for a long time, but certain events and situations may trigger your overthinking. The trick here is to keep these strategies at the forefront of your mind to apply them to any situation that arises.

The one takeaway that I want you to have from this book is to dig deep and find out where your overthinking is coming from. Is it anxiety? Depression? Is it related to issues of self-esteem? Whatever it may be, figuring out the cause will help you pick the strategies within this book that you feel will prove most helpful to manage your specific situation. If your overthinking is caused by anxiety, utilizing CBT will be the best way to deal with it. If your overthinking happens because of self-esteem issues, practice meditation, and gratitude to combat it. The most effective way to help you manage your overthinking is to use as many strategies as possible. This way, you can figure out what is working for you and what isn't working. By doing this, you can spend your energy and time on perfecting the strategies that you've developed success with. Keep pursuing change and practicing the strategies that work for you. Changing yourself is a lifelong process, never give up!

If you enjoyed this book, a positive review on Amazon is welcome! I urge you not to give up and keep going even if you face failure. Overthinking is a manifestation of something deeper within you. Figure out what that is for you, and I promise that overcoming it will be an easier process than you think. Good luck!

www.ingramcontent.com/pod-product-compliance
Lightning Source LLC
Chambersburg PA
CBHW072030230526
45466CB00020B/1209